Discover Walden

SAFFRON WALDEN COUNTRYSIDE HISTORY AND WILDLIFE WALKS

Jacqueline Cooper

Routes by Peter Cooper

Original illustrations by Julie Lynne

This book is dedicated to the memory of
Gwendoline Mary Constance Cooper (1915-1994)

Produced by
COOPER PUBLICATIONS
24 Pelham Road, Clavering, Saffron Walden, Essex CB11 4PQ

This edition published 1996

ISBN 1 873669 01 1

By the same author:
Country Walks in Clavering (1987 – out of print)
Discover Clavering (1990 – available from publisher)

These walks were carefully checked prior to publication, but no
responsibility can be accepted by the authors/publishers for any changes
which may occur at a later date. All walks are undertaken at the walkers'
own risk and no responsibility can be accepted by the authors/ publishers
for any footpath problems encountered, which should be reported to the
Essex County Highways Department at County Hall, Chelmsford.

Printed by: Print Matters, Harlow (01279-302095)

Introduction

This book is a celebration of the countryside in and around the parish of Saffron Walden, in the form of walks with notes on the history and wildlife en route, including parts of the town where five of the nine walks begin. 'Discover Walden' has been a joint effort with my husband Peter, who has walked the paths at all four seasons to work out the best routes, negotiated for some footpath improvements, and contributed greatly to the many months of most enjoyable research. The wildlife notes are obviously subjective and transient but worth mentioning, for nature is the medium which links past and present. Walking is a wonderful therapy anyway, but every walk can come to life by pondering the names of wild flowers, the age of hedges, the origins of lanes, the sites of old settlements, the stories of past peoples, the names they gave to the fields. In this book an attempt has been made to relate the present-day landscape to some fine estate maps of the 1750s, themselves based on a Field Book of 1605. Mrs. D. Monteith's unpublished 1958 study of Saffron Walden is invaluable in understanding how this landscape evolved, while topographical descriptions by John Player, who published a book of walks from Saffron Walden in 1845, have been blended into the contemporary scene. In addition to some fine Victorian illustrations are 26 original charcoal drawings made especially for this book by Julie Lynne, an American visitor who captures an understanding of English countryside which we too often take for granted. The result of all this is a unique guide which we hope both residents and visitors will enjoy reading and exploring. This other Walden, the wider parish, is easily accessible, well farmed and good for wildlife. This is largely Ancient Countryside, where hedges and ponds, tracks and boundaries – were they compounded of bricks-and-mortar – would achieve grade-one listed status, but are so often undervalued. Antiquity is also to be perceived in that elusive something, an ephemeral whisper across centuries – felt momentarily in the breeze over the barley, the deep dark woodland silence, the rising song of skylark . Come, then, and explore the wider parish, come and 'Discover Walden' – and Ashdon!

Jacqueline Cooper

Using this Book

The sketch-maps are guides only, and not to any common scale. Walkers are recommended to buy the Ordnance Survey Pathfinder maps which cover Saffron Walden, TL 43/53 and TL 44/54. Paths designated thus ++++ are not necessarily rights-of-way, but seem to be in common usage. Essex County Highways Department is constantly improving the footpath network, which is largely signposted and well used so that none of the walks suggested are very difficult. There are several unavoidable road sections and walkers should TAKE EXTREME CARE on busy roads.

PUBLIC TRANSPORT: Buses operate along most of the busier roads but are infrequent. There is, however, an hourly town service in Saffron Walden. Most timetables are displayed at the High Street bus stop or can be obtained from the Tourist Information Centre. Essex Busline (0345 000333) is available daily with up-to-date timetables.

Symbols used

🌳	Woods	⇐ ⇒	**Turn left/right**
◼	Building	✳	**Site of interest**
------	Footpaths	～～～	**River**
══	Tracks	··········	**Parish boundary**
P	Parking		
+++++	Paths commonly walked but not rights-of-way		

Acknowledgements

Many people have been generous with their time and expertise, and particular thanks are expressed to: Roger Baron (County Highways); S.R. Bassett (archaeologist); Maureen Evans (Saffron Walden Museum); Martyn Everett (Town Library); Zofia Everett (Essex Record Office Archive Access Point); Julie Lynne; Margaret McGowan and other Ashdon walkers; Glenn Miller (Ashdon Museum); Joan Mummery (botanist); Saffron Walden Footpath Association; Sewards End Village Hall Committee; Tesco Stores; Beryl Thurgood (Sewards End); Malcolm White (Town Council); and others.

Contents

Illustrations

Drawings by Julie Lynne(JL) are available as limited prints. Write to address on page 86 for further information, quoting number: e.g. JL73.

Illustrations pp. 14 and 65 by courtesy of Saffron Walden Town Council.

Illustrations pp. 4, 6, 20, 28 and 52 by courtesy of Essex County Libraries, Trustees of the Saffron Walden Town Library.

Page 1- Almshouses(JL); 4 – Audley Park; 6 – Stone Bridge; 9 – Audley End; 10 – Church spire(JL); 11 – Castle Hill(JL); 14 – Buckenhoe Pond; 18 – The Slipes(JL); 20 – Saffron Walden Castle; 21 – Swan Meadow(JL); 22 – Bridge Street(JL); 28 – Littlebury Church; 30 – Windmill Hill(JL); 31 – Old Workhouse(JL); 32 – Ice Age boulder; 34 – Railway bridge(JL); 35 – Martinfield Green(JL); 36 – Aubery Field(JL); 38 – Old tractor(JL); 39 – Water Tower(JL); 43 – Thunderley Parsonage Farm(JL); 46 – The Roos; 48 – College of St Mark(JL); 50 – Wheat field(JL); 52 – Claypits; 55 – Beechy Ride(JL); 57 – Audley End Village(JL); 58 – St James Church(JL); 62 – Wills Ayley Lane(JL); 63 – Stocking Green(JL); 65 – Sewards End mill; 66 – Cloptons(JL); 67 – The Crown, Little Walden; 70 – Burntwood End Farm(JL); 73 – Old signpost(JL); 75 – Old gate; 76 – Ashdon Village Sign(JL); 77 – Ashdon Church; 82 – Rose and Crown(JL); 84 – Ashdon walkers; 85 – Ducks at Swan Meadow(JL).

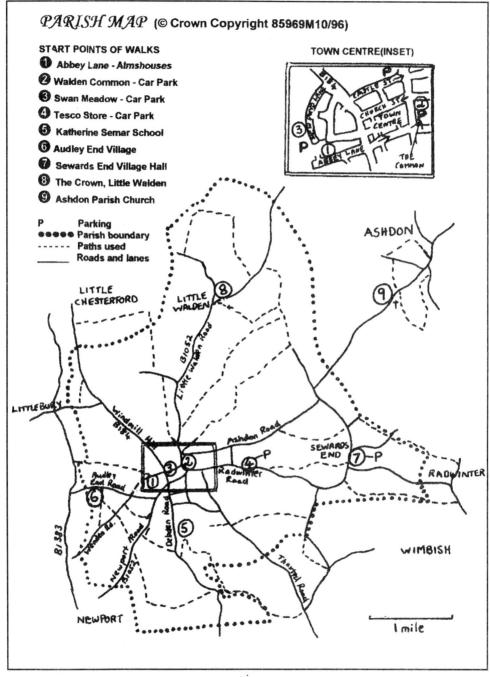

PARISH MAP (© Crown Copyright 85969M10/96)

START POINTS OF WALKS

1. Abbey Lane - Almshouses
2. Walden Common - Car Park
3. Swan Meadow - Car Park
4. Tesco Store - Car Park
5. Katherine Semar School
6. Audley End Village
7. Sewards End Village Hall
8. The Crown, Little Walden
9. Ashdon Parish Church

P   Parking
●●●●●   Parish boundary
- - - - -   Paths used
──────   Roads and lanes

TOWN CENTRE(INSET)

ASHDON

LITTLE CHESTERFORD

LITTLE WALDEN

LITTLEBURY

SEWARDS END

RADWINTER

WIMBISH

NEWPORT

1 mile

1 Audley End: 2½ miles

Begin at the beginning, the Abbey Lane area where, so far as anyone knows, the first proper settlement grew up at least 1,900 years ago, although earlier artefacts, from Stone, Bronze and Iron Ages have been found in other places too. There were Celtic villagers still here when the Saxons began arriving in the seventh century, for the early village is said to be named after them, 'weala denu', 'valley of the Britons'. The move uphill to the Castle area came later, in Norman times, but meanwhile a separate settlement grew up around Walden Abbey from the twelfth century onwards and this very popular walk encircles that area, fortunately never developed and remaining very rural and peaceful.

The King Edward VI Almshouses are very handsome though not actually the same ones named after the monarch in 1549, as a condition of the town charter, and where Samuel Pepys drank from a silver mazer bowl, scandalously later sold off. The buildings became dilapidated and were replaced last century with the help of philanthropic Quakers . In the original medieval almshouses, life was very strict – 'good rewle and clene levyng, non rebawdys, no chyderys, drunkelew ne latermakerys', they were told.

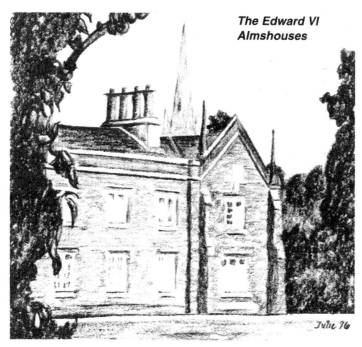

The Edward VI Almshouses

Julie 76

1

On the other side of Abbey Lane are the Repell Ditches, a deeply-banked hollow, dotted with snowdrops and aconites in late winter. This is all that remains of the magnum fossatum, which once extended almost right round the old town. Archaeologists did lots of digging round Walden in the 'Seventies and concluded that these remarkable earthworks were part of thirteenth-century town planning by Humphrey de Bohun, Lord of the Manor of Walden and Earl of Essex. Up till then, everyone thought they were prehistoric, understandably since Neolithic and Bronze Age flotsam has been found round about. So this was disappointing news, to find they were only 700 years old as the other theory would have made Walden a rarity indeed, a town whose layout was decided in prehistoric times. Many people prefer the earlier version, as a great historian once said, 'everything is older than we think'. The Abbey Lane area is awash with history for here too was the Saxon cemetery dug up in 1876,.producing Saffron Walden Museum's proudest possession, a beautifully-worked unique Viking necklace a thousand years old. Found amongst grave goods, this suggested pagan rites, whereas most of the 200 skeletons recovered were from Christian burials, dating back to the seventh century. This hugely important historical site, next to the Repell Ditches, now lies beneath the Gibson housing estate.

Before Hanover Place, at the end of the road was built, archaeologists had another dig and found prehistoric, Roman, Saxon and medieval material. Go past turreted Walden Lodge, through a gate into Audley End Park. To the right of the gateway was once a long-lost road, and another one lay ahead towards the Abbey itself, along what is now a tree-lined track(not a right-of-way.) This was the way the Benedictine monks walked to town 800 years ago, but the second Prior, Reginald opened a new road during redevelopment. Reginald, energetic and highly competent, dominated local life for 36 years and oversaw the Priory's elevation to Abbey in 1190, but died worn out.

The Abbey increased its wealth, a manorial domination which continued for centuries in its successor Audley End – by 1836 it was said that Lord Braybrooke owned two-thirds of the land in the parish. Even today, Audley End estates controls nine farms. But the riches of the monasteries were also their downfall, for Henry VIII coveted their treasures. Monks did sometimes contribute to their own demise, however – at Walden for instance the Abbot had secretly got married. In the sixteenth century, when there were just seven elderly monks left, the old foundation was dissolved, and today only Abbey Lane remains to echo 400 years of monasticism.

A Victorian writer, John Player was enamoured of this spot – 'we pass the row of young limes on either hand, dressed in their earliest shade of annual green... the grazing cattle in the pasturage around – the deer on the hill to the north, the fields...the thriving trees, the oak, the beech!' he exclaimed. People mock John Player's prose, but at least he left us a very valuable topographical record of Walden 150 years ago.

WALK 1: AUDLEY END

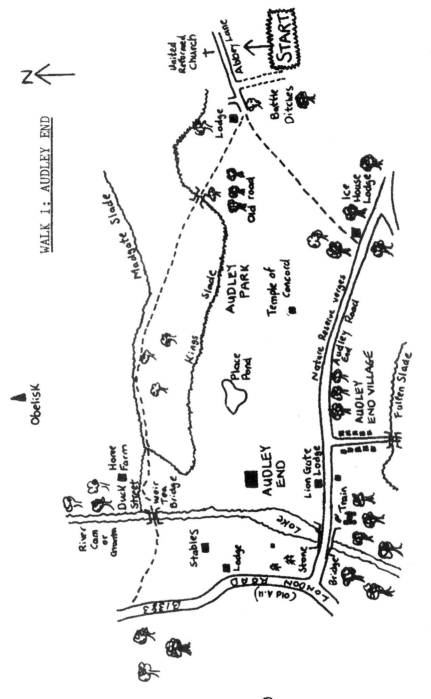

©Crown Copyright 85969M10/96

Audley Park in the nineteenth century(J.M. Youngman)

The park is still very beautiful, but much has changed – the deer park is no more, pastures were ploughed during the last war, many trees have gone. In Player's time the estate had already lost over 500 trees in an 1833 gale, while an 1896 'hurricane' uprooted many oaks, elms and an avenue of limes. The grand cedar of the Himalayas, the deodar up the hill, was perhaps just a sapling in the 1840s.

Following John Player's footsteps, turn left ⇐ from the gate, taking the right fork. Again these are ancient places, for along here have been found some little flint scrapers which Stone Age men used to clean animal skins. In those times, thousands of years ago, the entire population of Britain was perhaps only double that of Saffron Walden today, which is around 16,000. It seems amazing, therefore, to find anything Neolithic.

Artefacts of ancient date have also been found elsewhere in the park and, older still by several millennium, remains of woolly mammoth were discovered in the last century. It is a brief and pleasant stroll to the lodge opposite the Ice House, a sort of primitive fridge, in which ice from the lake was packed between straw in a deep well, to preserve foodstuffs for the gentry of the mansion. A well is referred to in the old field-name here, Holywell, although it can mean spring in a hollow. Holywell was once an open field between the Abbey and the town, enclosed into the park in the sixteenth century.

Turn right ⇒ out of the iron gate to Audley End Road – the trees over the way may be the same ones recorded as planted in 1787. Along the road is a designated Special Verge managed by Saffron Walden Town Council for the County Highway Authority. The long, tall wall – itself a listed ancient monument erected in the early seventeenth century – reflects the warmth of the sun, so that in wetter seasons one or two summer cuts are necessary to prevent coarse weeds crowding out the diverse sequence of flowers. These extend from bushes of the Duke of Argyll's Tea-tree at one end, down to the patches of Clary by the Lion Gate at the other. White Campion, Pyrenean Cranesbill and Pellitory-of-the-Wall precede long swathes of the pale mauve plumes and aromatic leaves of Lesser Calamint in late summer; and one or two isolated clumps of the stiff white-veined leaves of Star-of-Bethlehem can usually be detected.

This is the road which grew in importance after Prior Reginald closed the old one in the twelfth century. Large landowners had the privilege of executive decision, for instance a later lord of the manor in the 1780s used influence in the corridors of power to prevent a canal coming through his land – even though the townsfolk quite vociferously opposed him. The dispute left a lingering sense of bitterness, but a revised plan in 1810 also came to nothing. But would Saffron Walden be as attractive today, if it had developed a canal trade? Under commercial pressures, it would have lost something.

Along this road can be seen the site of a later Braybrooke campaign when, in 1833 the popular Audley End fair was moved from the greensward because it was 'a positive nuisance'. As chairman of the Bench he saw the worst of it – a Newport surgeon gaoled for 'acting riotously' in 1815, three lads whipped for picking pockets at the fair in 1828, another gaoled for gambling in 1832. And so the August fair moved to the Common, well away from his lordship.

It had been more respectable in the 1790s, wrote John Player, with 'cheese-stalls and gingerbread dealers – comparatively few people – great good humour – boughs projecting from the cottagers' homes, denoting that a glass of beer and a slice of ham might be had within – children blowing wooden trumpets, and holiday folk in holiday clothes... sober sedateness with lighthearted innocent jollity...'

Lighthearted innocent jollity is still available, however, on summer Sundays and bank holidays, on the miniature railway, a magical ride through teddybear-infested woodland, over Grandpa's Crossing and through Parson's Leap. Perhaps the bears, secretly nocturnal, are the only ones to get a glimpse of the spectral carriage said to drive out of the Lion Gate and up towards the Stone Bridge. The gate is named from the lion crest of the Howards, the family associated with Audley End for 200 years. Everything round here seems to be listed, Rickman's Lion Lodge, the 200-year-old wrought-iron railings along the road, and of course Adam's fine Stone Bridge of 1764, grade one quality, spanning the Granta. In 1813, a team of horses crashed through the bridge, but survived. During the last War, if Hitler had invaded, this bridge was wired up for explosion, a special chamber being built underneath for this purpose, part of a line of defensive ploys.

'Adam's fine Stone Bridge, spanning the Granta...'

No one can resist peeping over the parapets to watch the waterfowl, a lovely spot to lean and dream, by stately cedar and weeping willow. On one side a manicured lawn and perfectly edged lake, on the other in complete contrast a wild untidy streamside of sedge and weed where 'green and deep the stream mysterious glides beneath'. And compared to laid-back ducks and grazing geese on the other side, the birdlife this side is dynamic – here the woodpigeon flaps heavily, the deadly magpie flashes, a pair of spotted flycatchers boomerang in and out from a branch and, most excitingly, two flashes of blue mark a pair of kingfishers chasing each other downstream, skimming inches above the glimmering river! Two ways of managing landscape are bridged at this lovely spot: Audley End 'has not anything to show more fair'.

Turn right ⇒ along the old A11, perhaps following in the footsteps of the Saffron Walden Woolstaplers' Guild who, up until 1778, demonstrated their union solidarity with a ceremonial march every year out of town and back via parish boundary trees – oak and ash, elm and maple. They were celebrating the legendary Bishop Blaize, their patron saint. It was a big occasion, for sheep were important then – the Mayor and Corporation came too, with a band leading boy bishop, shepherds and shepherdesses in costume. The day ended with drinking and music and dancing.

And then there is the house, so well cared-for by English Heritage. It is impossible to go by here without glancing across and being enchanted. The well-known view of Audley End, reflected in Brown's still lake, never fails to catch the breath: whether cream and serene behind white-flannelled cricketers on some hazy summer afternoon; austerely white in the crisp clarity of winter; or bathed in gold in reflection of a westering sunset, when all the visitors have gone home. Notwithstanding the racetrack road, this is a pleasant walk past beautiful conifers – it is tempting to believe that Capability Brown planted them in the 1760s, but the historian Lord Braybrooke recorded that the Cedars of Lebanon west of the house were planted in 1827. It was Capability Brown, 'Lady Nature's second husband', who dramatically altered the grounds, replacing old formal gardens with his famous brand of informal landscaping. Those were busy days – much humping of soil, digging of gravel, levelling, draining and grubbing meant lots of work for townsfolk. The estate remained a big employer – in its heyday it took 50 gardeners to keep the place looking good, a dozen just to cut the grass – and no ride-on mowers then, nothing but scythes. Audley End was named after Henry VIII's Chancellor and Speaker of the House of Commons, Thomas Audley, granted the old Abbey in 1538 for help with certain unsavoury marital problems – he it was who helped Henry break away from Rome. Audley's successors, the Howards rebuilt it as a hugely expensive mansion, one of the biggest in the country, mostly now gone, for the building seen today is only a part of the original. For a period it was a Royal Palace, and royalty favoured Audley End, perhaps because they went away with a large gift of precious saffron – this was given to Elizabeth I in the sixteenth century, James I, Charles I, Charles II and William III in the seventeenth, Queen Anne,.George I and George III in the eighteenth century. By 1717, however, the Saffron Walden saffron industry was in terminal decline and the Corporation had to buy the stuff from Bishop's Stortford for their traditional present to King George!

History hits you between the eyes at Audley End – across the road atop a private hill is a prehistoric camp, known since the eighteenth century as Ring Hill. A new study in 1995 found it contemporaneous with Wandlebury, one of a series of Iron Age earthworks near this important north-south route along the Cam valley. Nearby is the patriotic Temple of Victory, designed in 1774 also by Robert Adam, to celebrate British triumph in the Seven Years War.

These memorials are dotted about all over the park to celebrate bits of history and to provide vistas. What would those careful Georgian designers have made of the concrete pillbox! The Cambridge gate and lodge on the right date from the 1760s, with fine chimneys and gateposts and the building behind was a stables, reflecting Braybrooke interest in racehorses – the site may originally have been the hostel where the Abbey gave hospitality to travellers. Had the canal scheme gone ahead, the course originally suggested would have run between this road and the Temple, ruining the vista so carefully composed by Capability Brown.

Turn right ⇒ (ignoring a 'private' sign) down a signposted farm track, past walls of flint – further down the gardens of Audley End can be glimpsed over the wall, and the columns of the grade-one listed, eighteenth-century Tea House Bridge. Another bridge, beside an attractive wildlife area, crosses the Granta which, like its other name Cam is said to be Scandinavian in origin – Essex came under the Danelaw in the late ninth century. An early documentary reference, in 1248, simply calls it 'riveram de Waledena'. This unassuming little waterway has seen so much, for this was the way the earliest peoples came, Neolithic hunter-gatherers whose sheep and goats left fleeting traces of their stay on the fertile riverside terraces. Later from the same northern direction came Bronze Age voyagers, using the river as the easiest route into the deep Essex forest.

Whereas the present main road runs only to the west of the river, there was also an early road on the east side, presumably near the present farm. This was once an important 'king's highway' from Cambridgeshire to Newport and beyond, and along this section, Duck Street, a seventeenth century map shows 16 cottages, a little hamlet specifically built to house workers on the estate, with watermills along the river. The Abbey had been sited deliberately at the meeting point of four roads, for the benefit of poor travellers but, with Dissolution, the old roads inevitably declined. The sweeping changes on the estate in the eighteenth century – rebuilding, landscaping, extending.– included the final stopping up of this very ancient route, which dated back at least to Roman times.

Follow a waymark to the right ⇒ along an earth track around the flint walls. Through a kissing gate and a brick archway lie lovely meadows, Park Bottoms, between the.Madgate Slade, earlier the Walden Brooke, and the King's Slade. Across to the left is the former Deer Park, used as venue for the Essex Show in 1860, 1870 and 1884. These meadows were another favourite place where John Player 150 years ago would 'saunter undisturbedly by the margin of the separating stream, but cheered by its rippling contributions to the harmony – the natural harmony – of the morning hour.' Local slades seem diminished now, but an early name for the middle meadow, Watering Place and a path called the Causeway underline how boggy this area was in earlier times – hence the siting of the Abbey on higher drier ground.

It may be fanciful to imagine the survival of a venerable oak recorded by Lord Braybrooke in 1836, 14 feet round and 60 feet high, planted in 1720. But the oaks dotted about are very fine and this is still, as in the last century, a place to linger, soothed by birdsong, squinting in the sunlight at distant monuments to the great and good of the eighteenth century – an obelisk for a countess, a temple for a king: today we are content with coronation seats and jubilee trees – they thought big in those days. Another waymarked kissing gate leads to a track by the sewage works, where part of a shield, medieval scalloped horseshoes and Roman Samian ware were once found. If only these artefacts could talk, then history would be less speculative!

Over a wooden footbridge in the next field stands a beautiful beech tree above which in high summer 'gathering swallows twitter in the skies', gliding higher or lower depending on humidity, the better to catch their prey. Our little journey today can scarcely compare to the one they will soon take back to Africa. Yet this short stroll, a favourite with generations of townsfolk, captures the essence of Saffron Walden's historical heritage, and it is pleasant on Sunday afternoons to end up at the Abbey Lane church hall for tea and cakes, raising money for refugees in less happy lands whose own history has been destroyed.

Audley End in the nineteenth century (J.M. Youngman)

Saffron Walden Church Spire

2 Byrds and Butlers: 4¹/₂ miles

The Common is Saffron Walden's village green, once called the Greene, a former meadow where the burgesses had grazing rights. At the top a drinking fountain for a queen, at the bottom the largest earthen maze in north-west Europe, one mile long. In 1739 the great evangelical preacher, George Whitefield preached in the outdoors here to a crowd of 2000. In 1814 2,600 townsfolk prematurely celebrated the end of the Napoleonic Wars – but even more, some 4,000 sat down for Victoria's jubilee dinner in 1897, requiring 959 yards of tablecloth. This greensward has also withstood the feet of Napoleonic cavalry, the planting of commemoratory trees, the digging of air-raid shelters and the controversial car park built in 1954. There was almost a railway station here in the 1840s but 'Common' sense prevailed. Domestic uses were also discouraged: 'the busy bustling housewives of the town send forth their household linen to be blown about, much to the alarm of timid horsemen and wayward cattle', complained a local worthy in 1843. But people have danced and sledged, attended fairs, sports, services, dinners and celebrations time out of mind. The Common reverberates with community, it belongs to the people.

'The shady, flint-walled path along Castle Hill...'

11

Turn right ⇒ from the car park and walk up the grass to the top of the Common, opposite which there is an interesting juxtaposition of rich man's castle and poor man's church: the butchers' shop occupies a nineteenth century Primitive Methodist Chapel – from this building a distinctive medium of Christianity was missioned out to over 70 local villages in its heyday. The Primitives were the working peoples' church. After spending six days labouring in the fields, their poor and semi-literate local preachers would take to the roads on their day off, to visit village chapels and barns and spread the word of the Lord in simple terms among the rural poor. Always they were hamstrung by the sheer poverty of the 'aglabs' who made up most of their membership and 'could not pay their class monies while children were wanting bread which the parents had not to give them.' Thus the reality of the Victorian rural idyll.

One of Walden's special little corners is the shady, flint-walled path along Castle Hill, with distant views of fields. Turn right ⇒ along tree-lined Pound Walk, near where stray animals were once impounded in Little Walden Road. This continues as Sheds Lane, named after Thomas Shed who once held an acre in Bucknoe Lane.

Historically-minded councillors have commemorated local history in street names: De Bohun Court recalling the man who gave the town a charter in 1300, one of a famous family of landowners and warriors; other streets from the Howards and Nevilles, associated with Audley End for 400 years; Castle Cross was a place nearby, while Buckenhoe Road immortalises a field-name.

Field-names are fascinating artefacts in themselves, though hard to interpret – was it named after billy-goats, or from a man named 'Bucca'? The earliest record, Bukenhoslade in 1235, has topographical elements: Old English *hoh* describing a bank at the end of a ridge, and *slaed* meaning valley, a common word round Walden.

These were all steep fields one time, the view from them described by the Victorian writer John Player, as 'one of the most interesting amphitheatres that nature ever formed', and would be still if it wasn't for the 'ouses in between! But climb a little further and that view is still there.

Once into the fields there are vestiges of something John Player might still recognise, notwithstanding pylons and industrial units and food emporiums. Here still is his natural amphitheatre, 'rich with exquisite beauty... trees and hedges... clothed in their matchless attire... gentle airs that rustle the corn.. the happy lark bears it upward, in sweetest harmony...' and so on.

The massive blob of unscreened commerce and distant tinkle of ice-cream van intrude somewhat on this happy vision, but corn will always rustle and a skylark still bears it upwards, at certain times of year. The skylark, beloved of poets, is now on the danger list of threatened birds, but still they 'tremble there, a nerve of song' over Walden fields. A more secretive warbler chirrups in a bush, aristocrat butterflies dance in search of nectar and now, as then, Pounce, Grimsditch, Westley and the Audley End woods lie distant dark shapes.

WALK 2: BYRDS & BUTLERS

This could be Player's 'matchless' hedgerow, regenerating with some dozen species, including oak, ash, willow, maple, hazel, crab and wayfaring tree. He also praised Rickman's then-new addition to the landscape, the magnificent church spire, completed in June 1832, soaring to 193 feet. It is said to be the largest church in Essex, rebuilt on the wealth of wool in Tudor times. On almost every walk, because Walden sits in 'a valley, beautifully embosomed with hills', that lovely spire is a beacon spearing the sky, guiding the lost in more ways than one.

Although these have been big empty fields for some time, there may have been settlement up here in the past – the Buckenhoe Barn was a known landmark, now gone, but an old pond remains, usually taken as a sign that someone lived here once. Recent field-walking has revealed prehistoric and Roman sites just by here. The pond is fed by a spring – in the 1840s Player commented that the spring had water enough to supply the town, but nowadays it scarcely fills the pond. Still the old pond supports iris, reeds, Celery-leaved Crowfoot and aromatic Water Mint. And still, as shown in John Youngman's fine water-colour, 'the view all around embraces many miles – it is truly capacious', the church spire rising in the valley below.

Buckenhoe Pond in the nineteenth century (J.M. Youngman)

14

The land falls away from this high point and, although so near the town, this is a very peaceful walk, part of the Harcamlow Way long-distance route. In a dry summer grasshoppers leap ahead on the grassy track and the lovely oaks offer welcome shade. The waymarked path veers left ⇐, along an old boundary, where a deep ditch offers a succession of flora, in spring Cowslips and Stitchwort, topped with white sloe blossom and lemon willow catkins, in summer St. John's Wort and tall Teasels with their attendant butterflies and moths. Wild roses are, however, doing a take-over job, some decorated with the red growths of robins' pincushions, inside which lives a gall wasp: this can be parasitised by another species of wasp, which in turn gets eaten up by yet another species. This is what is meant by the old expression, 'Nature red in tooth and claw'. An ivy-covered staghead oak offers habitat even in death to a myriad creatures, and there are wide views of distant wooded hills across vast fields, now silent and still, where once the air would have been filled with 'the sound of sheep unshepherded' when Bucknoe sheepwalk stretched 120 acres wide. At that time these fields would have been down to grass, and are said to have been the venue for pony races, for which the Corporation gave a silver cup. Later on they were converted to arable and achieved another footnote in history: when, in July 1795, the people of Walden took to the streets to protest about the price of bread, the rioters 'threatened that as soon as the corn was up on a place called Buckenhall Leys, they would go and cut it and the wives should carry it away.' There were bread riots in many places that year and their legacy was an enduring one. Attitudes to the poor were never quite the same again.

Dip gently downhill, past another hedge and, in the sheltered bottom beside a waymark post, and hidden beneath a brambly copse, lies one of those ancient field ponds so valuable for wildlife: gungey and log-strewn, inhabited by mallard, shaded by chestnut and weeping willow. It is a sign of benign landownership to see such things left alone, untidied, undisturbed. A solitary dying oak stands in the field to the right, which was once wood pasture. The recommended route here is straight ahead, up the hill, past the old brick garden wall of Byrds Farm, its warmth and the late nectar offered by ivy attracting perhaps a speckled wood butterfly. The little copse hides a pheasant area with a larger pond, popular with mallard, moorhen and white ducks.

Where the gravel track goes off to the left, turn right ⇒ along a track, which appears on old maps to be a remnant of a major east-west route of great antiquity, called Holmer Cross Lane. A poet once said that 'roads go on, while we forget and are forgotten', but in fact many old lanes and paths shown on the 1750s estate maps of Walden have completely disappeared, their *raison d'etre* redundant. Sometimes, though, we can still walk in ways trod for a thousand years or more.

There is still much woodland in these uplands – in spring Little Grimsditch Wood over yonder shines with white sloe blossom. In Saxon times much of this land was wooded, Great Bears Wood named after its use as pannage for swine, not a good thing since it stopped woods regenerating. There are hares about, and the verges and ditches are colourful with butterflies and wild flowers, including a patch of Lucerne, important in past pasture. A large oak here offers opportunity to try out the dating theory, that free-standing trees add approximately one inch in girth each year, which, measured at breast height, suggests it is 150 years old.

After this, the track bears right ⇒ beside a deep ditch. Beside a gas board sign is a gap over the ditch – here turn left ⇐ just before Ten Acre Wood and follow the sinuous, ditched and banked woodland edge, signs of ancient woodland since more recent plantations seldom have these features. Among a rich variety of trees are oak, hornbeam, maple and ash and shrubs include chalk-loving dogwood; spindle, its candy pink poisonous berries prominent in winter; and honeysuckle in its wild form, woodbine.

The actual right of way is across the field following the power lines, probably once a Roman route. But it is easier to continue left ⇐ along a hedge which, left uncut till late winter, offers wildlife an autumn feast of hazelnuts and haws and sloes. Pausing at the bottom to look back, there comes a momentary impression that all this has happened before, the woodpigeons and crows in the treetops, a hare leaping, the gentle swish of the breeze rippling upwards across the corn, green in spring, bronzed in summer, waves rolling towards a forested shore. The feeling of timelessness is reinforced by the Tudor field name, Abbots Layes, a link with Walden Abbey eight centuries ago, for this was part of their demesne. And there are older things – a Roman road probably passed near here.

Turn right ⇒ at the bottom through a gap, over a single-plank wooden bridge and along a sloe hedge to the left. Across to the right, beyond the conifers, is a field called in Tudor times Castells Pavie, appearing to derive from Saxon words, 'castel' meaning stones and *pavis* meaning defence: this was once thought to be the site of a manor but there is no evidence of this, and no one knows what it might mean. The name Crabbtree Rasers, one of several pastures amidst the woods, is self-explanatory, a reminder that the making of cider is known to have happened even in prehistoric times.

Turn left ⇐ after 150 yards, to go along an ancient common lane following the telegraph lines, up to Butlers Farm, which name goes back to a twelfth century knight, Geoffrey le Boteler who leased the land as a sub-manor of the demesne. The present house dates to 1610, the same period of Audley End House. These peaceful fields were the scene of great drama in the early hours of 19 April 1944, when the only wartime plane to crash in Walden parish came down here, disintegrating on impact. Two of the German crew of the Heinkel 177, shot down by a Mosquito, were killed and four taken prisoner. Part of the last major air raid on London, this was one of 13 losses among the 53 enemy planes which reached England. The site of the crash was in the field on the right of this path.

Looking back to the wooded distance, it is still possible – in spite of nineteenth century enclosure, elimination of pasture and modern agricultural revolution – to discern the medieval pattern of farming, the landscape of *bocage* – of small enclosed fields of different sizes, mixed in with little woods, winding hedgerows, and old tracks, what we think of as an English landscape but also typical of parts of Normandy. It is very different from the *champaign*, the big open chalky fields to the south of town, for in these upland woody parts, land had to be strenuously assarted bit by bit from the forest – the Saxon field-names, Reddings and Stockins describe the clearance process. Field archaeologists now say, however that this is not the whole story, that such woodland might simply have grown over abandoned Roman farmland and needed clearing again centuries later.

Reaching the barns of Butlers, turn left ⇐ under electricity cables, and then left ⇐ again along a grassy byway, a continuation of Butlers Lane. This is an old way, travelled in time – Tudor maps call it 'the way from Linton to Suardsend', and it connects all the big farms along its way, but is now mostly byway or bridleway. There is such antiquity in these old roads! And they are full of wildlife – butterflies enjoy a sunny stand of nettles and thistles, invertebrates galore live in an old staghead oak, a kestrel hovers. And there are very fine hedges, well cared-for and reflecting the chalkier soil with dogwood and wayfarers tree prominent. In their quiet, warm shelter flourish masses of Cowslips in spring.

Hedges are very special things, corridors for wildlife, often much older than they seem, and useful to farmers, for they harbour predators which consume cereal pests. Recent Parliamentary proposals would protect all old boundary, archaeological, ecologically-rich and many other special hedges, including those with seven or more woody species per 30 metres. Overgrown hedges have been described as 'hardly hedge-rows, little lines of sportive wood run wild' and these have their place; but a well-managed farm hedge like this, tall and thick, the berries left till the end of winter, is probably even better, particularly if cut only every two years by something kinder than a bushwhacker!

Turn left ⇐ at a break in the hedge along another grassy old way, once known as Sewats Lane, presumably after some cottager of long ago. There are some more fine oaks, lively with the sound of long-tailed tits in search of the many insects which live on these trees. And there are others, older craggy things with hollow middles but still very much alive. Time stands still, beneath these oaks, the smell of new-ploughed earth after harvest wafting over on the breeze. While hedge bottoms imitate lost woodland – for Dog's Mercury and Lesser Periwinkle were originally woodland plants – the verges echo vanished meadows, with Cowslips in abundance.

After a long, sinuous, flat and grassy walk, there is a waymark downhill on a reinstated path towards a gap in the spinney. This is yet another place once settled, long abandoned, known once as Halegreene, now just a few bricks in the stream, a broken bridge, amid overgrown coppice. Cross the footbridge at the Slipes, pause awhile to savour the silence, sit on a fallen log, part of a very ancient oak still green and growing, in spite of its big split heart An old metal footpath sign has survived, broken, but still pointing the way to Little Walden.

Old oak and signpost at The Slipes

Turn right then left ⇐ at a waymark along a hedge up to Grimsditch Wood, its sinuous outlines little changed over centuries, an ancient woodland of great beauty. Recent field-walking has revealed that there was prehistoric farming in the fields around the wood, but other archaeologists have even more recently declared that old earthworks, long thought to be Iron Age, were simply part of medieval woodland management. It is hard to accept this as the whole story, for there is an atmosphere hereabouts: 'the howes of the silent vanished races' seem tangible. It is known, at any rate, that there was Roman activity, for Samian ware, glass, iron and other artefacts, originally buried in a chest and dug up in 1844, can be seen at Saffron Walden Museum. The modern name Grimsditch is misleading, a corruption of the early name, Grimswhych, derived from a once-common Essex surname, plus the Saxon word *wic* meaning dairy-farm.

Old oakwoods, carpeted in bluebells, are a superb habitat for wildlife, popular with birds and butterflies, and inhabited by rabbits, hares, pheasants, deer and other animals. Helping themselves to these riches was a rural habit but attitudes hardened over time: whereas in 1395 a man was fined 4s.3d. at the manor court for 'allowing his beasts to trespass in the lord's wood of Grimswhych'; almost 500 years later, in 1834, someone was put to one month's hard labour on the treadmill at Chelmsford Gaol, a dreadful punishment, just for 'damaging and destroying the underwood in Grimswood'.

Turn left ⇐ at a waymark walking beside a hedge until level with Byrds Farm. Although an eighteenth century building, there are some older barns, and the farm was in the Byrd family at least two centuries before. The Byrds were an ancient Walden family – there was a Thomas Byrd in 1400 who helped to found the almshouses, another whose land was taken away in Cromwell's time, and as recently as 1929, when the Almshouse Mazer bowl was sold, one protester was Henry Llewellyn Bird, descendant of that medieval Thomas. As a settlement, the site is even older, for some unusual rings thought to be Saxon loom weights, as well as pottery, were once dug up nearby.

After the hedge ends, it is replaced by a barbed wire fence – look out for a stile on the right ⇒ cross this, then a second stile, past the house and right ⇒ onto the farm road. There are some pretty gardens to admire, continuing downhill to where the road forks. Ignore the right-hand fork, once part of a medieval or older lane but now private. Turn left ⇐ ahead down Byrds Farm Lane past pond, midden, and tall hedges. It is possible to do this entire walk and see never a soul till reaching Byrds Farm Lane where the skylark returns to sing the weary walker homewards on an ancient lane preserved through the modern housing estates.

When the houses off Little Walden Road were built, councillors resurrected the nicer field-names, Fairleas and Sweet Mead – curiously, none are named after a small field which used to lie back where the path forked, Cucold Acre – this translates as 'a secluded piece of land favoured for illicit lovemaking'! The mind boggles. Usterdale Road was named after Oyster Dane, rising steeply to the left, so called in 1400, valley of sheepfolds, from a Saxon word *eowestre*; further down was damper land, in a triangular shape, hence the seventeenth century name Morisses Harpe, while to the right the land rises on a former open field, Doddenhill, another reference to woodland.

Nearby were the Limekiln allotments, the first ones laid out under the pioneering spade husbandry scheme in 1830 where, for a rent of fourpence or fivepence a rod, industrious labourers were encouraged, distinguished from 'the men of idle habits who are of necessity sent for occupation into the public roads.' Saffron Walden was probably the first town in the country to adopt this idea. But it was not entirely altruistic – the elite had their reasons, largely to do with improving the habits of the poor and reducing their own rate bills.

These are the lands where woolly mammoth roamed some 14,000 years ago – a mammoth tusk, found in a gravel pit near Little Walden Road, is a prize exhibit in the Saffron Walden Museum, worth a visit at the end of this walk, by turning left ⇐ at the end of the path back to town. Beside the Museum are the remains of Saffron Walden Castle, built in the twelfth century, probably by the de Mandeville who also got the town its original market, at Newport's expense. The castle did not last long, and much of the original stone was probably re-used for road-mending, although part was still used as a stable in the last century.

From a distance the Castle looks a grade-one listed shapeless heap, but has its own charms at close hand. Not least, the crumbling walls offer life to self-seeded Wallflowers, a species thought to have arrived in England via imported stone from Caen in Norman times. They were recorded in the castle walls at least 150 years ago. There is also a fine view from the Castle hill, from which it is pleasant to sit and imagine how it might have looked over eight centuries ago when the town moved from the Abbey Lane area to this higher, safer vantage-point.

Saffron Walden Castle in the nineteenth century (J.M. Youngman)

3 Springwell & Littlebury: 5½ miles

Swan Meadow was always the damp end of town, its water-table so high that the peat below preserved remains of prehistoric ox and deer and wild horse up to 10,000 years old. Archaeologists have recently found traces of the Repell Ditches which extended under what is now car park. They never found any fossil of a legendary venomous serpent, which lurked in the Meads and killed half the population, including a brave knight who died defending them! Largely undeveloped, the area became, until 1992, overgrown grassland, actually rare ancient wet pasture habitat, the haunt of snipe and heron. At least 54 species of birds were recorded here, including owls, swift, woodpecker, nuthatch, goldcrest, siskin and kingfisher, as well as 72 types of plants, 11 different mammals, 17 butterfly species and much else besides. It is still incomprehensible to nature-lovers that all this untidy natural beauty was sacrificed to the car, but a little remains – some grassland, an old weeping willow, the New Pond. It has been well-landscaped with hundreds and hundreds of new trees and shrubs thriving, and Swan Meadow is a pleasant spot to sit and watch the ducks. Possibly a hygienic, parkland concept and not an ancient meadow, but that seems to be what most people prefer.

The New Pond at Swan Meadow

21

From the (prepaid) car park go ahead towards the church spire, over the footbridge and turn left ⇐ beside mellow brick walls and the remnants of Swan Meadow, above which swallows still wheel and glide. On the right, just before the houses, is the Monks' Door through which the monks of Walden Abbey are said to have passed on their way to town. Freshwell Street, which takes its name from the Hundred of Freshwell, is full of gems – the jettied timber-frame of Fearns, the oval windows of Freshwell House, the Almshouse Tenements given by George Stacey Gibson in 1881, interspersed with 'twitchells', the local name for these intriguing little alleys. Emerge opposite the Eight Bells, where it is worth a detour right to look at the grade-one listed Youth Hostel. Otherwise cross the road and turn left ⇐ down Bridge Street, again full of attractive houses – in one of these the short-lived silk crepe industry originated in the last century.

Looking down Bridge Street from the Youth Hostel

Lord Braybrooke paid for the bridge over the Slade, but flooding continued to be a problem, since the hills around send their water down here. It was so bad in the 1790s that people took to rafts, and in August 1917 water lay four feet deep in this road, trapping people in their homes. As recently as 1960 there were more floods.

At the end, turn right ⇒ along a signposted path between Bridge End Farm barns, to be converted into houses, and the allotments: Saffron Walden pioneered allotments in the 1830s, one of their organisers exclaiming: 'Oh, how admirable they look! How like one large garden! What a sweet feature in the landscape!' And jolly hard work, after a day spent labouring in the fields. But the allotments were credited with keeping Walden labourers peaceful when 'Captain Swing' riots disrupted the local countryside in 1830. Only the 'respectable' labourers were allowed to have them though.

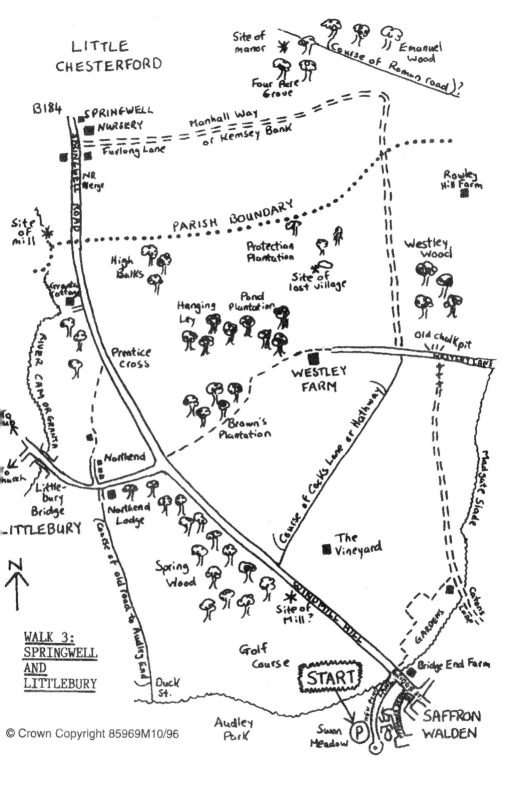

LITTLE
CHESTERFORD

Site of manor

Four Acre Grove

Course of Roman road?

Emanuel Wood

B184

SPRINGWELL NURSERY

Manhall Way or Kemsey Bank

Furlong Lane

NR Verge

Site of mill

Rowley Hill Farm

PARISH BOUNDARY

High Balks

Protection Plantation

Westley Wood

Site of lost village

Ingrebe Cottage

Old chalk pit

RIVER CAM OR GRANTA

Hanging Ley

Pond Plantation

PLOVER'S LANE

Prentice Cross

WESTLEY FARM

Church

Littlebury Bridge

LITTLEBURY

Northend

Brown's Plantation

Course of Cocks Lane or Hathway

Madgate Slade

Northend Lodge

The Vineyard

Course of old road to Audley End

Spring Wood

Gardens

Colvin's Close

Site of mill?

WINDMILL HILL

Golf Course

Bridge End Farm

WALK 3:
SPRINGWELL
AND
LITTLEBURY

Duck St.

Audley Park

Swan Meadow

P

NEW ROAD

BRIDGE ST

SAFFRON WALDEN

N

© Crown Copyright 85969M10/96

Another enduring legacy of philanthropy are the Bridge End Gardens, behind ivy-covered walls, landscaped In Victorian times and recently restored after gale damage in 1990. Continue round the cricket field, laid out on a meadow belonging to the old Catons Lane Farm; then turn right ⇒ beside a garden, with chickens pecking about.

Turn left ⇐ at a signpost, up Catons Lane, known earlier as Westlie waye, a wide grassy track past a solitary oak. The Madgate Slade, here seldom more than a dry stream-bed, meanders on one side, and on the left is a field which retains a name over a thousand years old: in Saxon times it was Coppid bush, suggesting woodland maintained as coppice: by 1600 it was Cockbushfeilde, arable open field divided into strips for cultivation. A track which once ran across it was called Cockebushwaye. Looking back, there is a fine view of the town, with the familiar church spire, then the open track narrows to run between hedge and a high bank, probably formed by centuries of ploughing down the slope of Cock Bush Field – oxen needed a wide turning area, and so the plough board pushed soil into lynchets, which over time formed raised banks at field edges. The hedgerow seems old, including spindle, dogwood, maple and wayfaring tree which enjoy chalky soil. The method of hedge-dating, by counting species, suggests it may have been planted in Tudor times, and documentary research confirms that this boundary was in existence by 1600.

Keep ahead through a gap in the hedge, now on a field-edge path with the bank falling away steeply to the right before levelling out again. Ahead lies Westley Wood, which may be ancient woodland, although in 1605 it was called Westlie grove, which suggests a plantation. Around the wood, south-east and north-east, ancient settlement sites have recently been identified, one Iron Age, another Roman. Field-walkers, looking for concentrations of pottery sherds, are convinced that prehistoric farming was widespread, which means that our traditional picture of impenetrable forest persisting till Saxon times is misleading. The land has not always been this empty, for *everything is older than we think.*

So it is not unlikely that a place like Westley Farm, documented as a thirteenth century sub-manor leased to John de Westlee, had an earlier existence as a settlement. Again recent field-walking has found concentrations of Saxon and Norman sherds nearby. The farm is to the left ⇐ along Westley Lane past an old chalkpit, along a surfaced track. An old lost lane nearby, linking Westley with Butlers, was Holmerscrosseway, deriving from a Scandinavian word *holmr* meaning high dry ground – good reason for choosing a place to live. Although it lacked the status of its own manor court, the farm grew and flourished, with large sheepwalks in the seventeenth century. Inside Westley Farm is said to have once possessed a haunted cupboard! Before reaching the farm, turn right ⇒ following the Springwell signpost, a steady climb on a wide grassy track with one very old ash tree.

In these lonely fields, the art and drama and music of nature seem more tangible: for art is a floral tapestry of blue, yellow, pink and white right through the spring and summer, in chalky ditch and grassy bank. In May there are hundreds of Cowslips, sometimes called Pegles or more fancifully St Peter's Keys, for on the spot where St Peter dropped the keys of heaven, there sprung up these nodding golden bells. It is impossible not to be enchanted by Cowslips: 'there lives the dearest freshness deep down things'. Drama is in the landscape near and far: hares leaping the corn at front-stage, against a backcloth of 'blue remembered hills', the Chilterns ending gently amidst the East Anglian Heights. And music is birdsong, a soaring skylark on top of the world spilling 'rubbed and round pebbles of sound' in perfect pitch; and the cuckoo adding a deeper note from distant woods.

Gradually the ditchbank becomes more shrubby and could easily become a hedge again – here are willow, sloe, bramble, elder, dogwood, rose, hawthorn, hazel regenerating all along. A survey of 1400 shows that this boundary existed then, so these may possibly be the remnants of a medieval hedgerow. Three centuries ago, it was all sheepwalk up here, vast enclosed areas of permanent grassland – the element *ley* in field-names here refers to old sheep country, as Cotelaye, on both sides of this path.

Notwithstanding marching pylons, the spirit of ancient places remains: the hedgerow to the left of a gap blends into a wider, denser parish boundary hedge, where the beating of the bounds took place in another age. This boundary was moved further north some centuries ago from its former line. An old estate map gives it a name, Foxburrow Way.

We may imagine it has always been this quiet, this otherworldly, the realm only of rabbits and pheasants, but not so. Once again field-walking confounds the common view, identifying a Roman, possibly Iron Age, settlement site across to the left near what is now Protection Plantation. In medieval times, this plateau high above the valleys was also the site of yet another sub-manor, Bollesgrove which apparently had its own handy hamlet of attached peasants known as Eynesend, identifiable now only by a pond or two used for water supply.

Further along this path lies another old pond, touched by the parish boundary, decorated with Bluebells, a legacy of woods, and Cowslips, a ghost of meadows, and the nocturnal footprints of visiting creatures. It lies half-hidden within a fine ash/oak hedgerow, possibly an important boundary, the big bank a clue to antiquity, reflecting generations of ploughing building up the soil. The ditch then deepens and its bank, opening out away from shady hedgerows, once again supports many wild flowers.

But then the countryside alters again – always surprises in this fascinating landscape. The hedges are gone and big chalky open fields cascade down the hill. Turn left ⇐ down another wide track, Manhall way, sometimes called Kemsiewaye, beside which a white slope of ploughed-up chalk contrasts with the dark shape of Emanuel Wood above.

Anyone walking down here on 30 May 1944 would be lucky to survive, for hot metal rained from the skies! There was an ammunition dump, chock full of bullets, grenades, mines and even mustard gas crazily sited in Emanuel Wood right near a hospital in Little Chesterford Park. A series of explosions led to the mass evacuation of patients, windows were smashed for miles around including Walden, thatch set on fire, trees flattened and the noise heard as far away as Ely. It was said to be caused by a discarded cigarette. The Bomb Disposal Squad still comes, half a century on, to periodically deal with dangerous fragments.

There are much older associations, too. Near here ran once a Roman road from Chesterford down to Radwinter, touching on Little Walden. A few Roman sherds have been found in the wood and, on aerial photographs, there lurk spectral trails of disturbed soil. But otherwise the well-built ways down which armoured legions marched 2,000 years before are gone as if they had never been.

This pleasant downhill track, by Pegle-dotted banks had a different and much later purpose, as access road to yet another long-lost chunk of the past, a Saxon manor. This site, which cannot be seen from the path as it lies over the hill behind trees, was a vanished moated manor house of great antiquity known as Manhall, its name taken from a Saxon word *gemaene*, appropriately translating as manor house on a parish boundary – this was in the time when the Walden boundary was further north. Archaeologists have discovered evidence of settlement from the tenth to the twelfth centuries. At Domesday Monehala, as it then was, was part of the lands held by Siward, the same man from whom Sewards End is named. By the seventeenth century the old building was in ruins, and now all trace has gone. Emanuel Wood, which seems to be a corruption of Manhall Woods, has reduced in size.

The track was also access to the wide, sweeping open fields which prevailed here, a type known as *champaign*, dramatically different from the woody *bocage* in some parts of Walden parish. The strip-field system, so often described, can readily be imagined upon these interlocking slopes, divided into pieces called furlongs, the furrows changing direction with the change of slope. Even modern machinery must find these slopes a challenge, and in past times they were even more difficult, as noted in a survey of 1600: 'There is much of the worst sort of lande in Springwelle, in Cockebushfielde, in Kemesey banke'. Lower down Manhall Way used to be called Furlong Lane, descending now past Springwell Nursery. Springwell, formerly Joseph Farm, is part of Audley End Estates. Quite recently a hand grenade from the Emanuel Wood explosion was found here. Until the early twentieth century, Springwell was a detached part of Walden, and nomansland, judging by a dispute in 1824 when Walden and Little Chesterford officials argued as to who should repair the road. The name may refer to exceptional springs.

An old field-name here is Gallow Croft up the road, which may have some manorial connection, but was probably not used much – the right to a gallows was a medieval status symbol! There are also signs of Scandinavian influence in some of the field-names around this area, particularly down by the Granta.

How useful it would be to be able to walk along that old river as did Neolithic, Bronze Age and Danish explorers, but alas this is not possible. Therefore there is no avoiding some annoying road-walking, apart from visiting Springwell Nursery while waiting for a bus. Turn left ⇐ from the Nursery near which is a nature reserve wild flower verge. Cross the road to the opposite verge for the next half-mile. *There is no pavement joining the Springwell and the Littlebury footpaths and the road is a racetrack, therefore walkers should stay on the verge and take great care.*

About a quarter-mile along, the present parish boundary crosses the main road, to the left of the plantation, High Balks. To the right, opposite here, is the site of a former watermill, Farynworth, hence the field known as Mill Hern. Just beyond here is a driveway to Granta Cottage, and on a bit further a waymarked telegraph pole marking an otherwise unsigned track which used to be an ancient and important road.

Turn right ⇒ along this track, which was the old 'road to Audley End', from a spot known in Tudor times as Prentis Cross. Field-names on a farm map of 1752 offer a clue to past activities – to the harvesting of oziers for baskets, rushes for floor-coverings, hops for ale. An area then known as The Nursery forms now a woody dell full of rabbits and there were humpy meadows, where sheep still graze. The ancient way now forms a pleasant, wide grassy track, alive with grasshoppers and busy bees. At the end are some attractive estate cottages dated 1873.

In Tudor times there was a small settlement near where the track emerges opposite Northend Lodge through which the old road, closed in the seventeenth century, once continued on through Duck Street, Audley Park, Audley End Village, Abbey Farm, over the Walden-Wenden road and beyond. The Audley End kennels used to be at Northend, where the gamekeeper enjoyed quite a reputation for the excellence of his dogs.

As in many of these little hamlets, there was great poverty here in the nineteenth century – in 1862 the Saffron Walden Town Missionary reported on a family he visited at Northend: 'they had six children and her husband had only nine shillings per week... cannot obtain any assistance by way of charity as they are between two parishes... they do not allow anything from the Parish... she belonged to Walden and her husband belonged to Littlebury...' Woe betide those without a parish!

From here a diversion could be taken to look at Littlebury, by turning right⇒ past the decorative Lodge with its unusual chimneys and down to the River Granta – in Littlebury once known as the Styric. The river, bridged beside the old watermill hung about with weeping willows, was the tragic end of a young deaf-and-dumb man who once drowned near here, unable to make anyone hear, recalled the Victorian writer, John Player, writing of 'the fair and goodly stream which on the left coquettes with the wheel of the mill' and flows north to join the Ouse to Ely. In the 1840s it was still just a ford with a footbridge, and had not changed since his boyhood in the 1790s.

Perchance the flora is the same too – big bold clumps of Burdock, Comfrey, and Himalyan Balsam, with patches of Lucerne and wild Hop clambering over the hedgerow, a survival from the mid-eighteenth century when hops were grown as a crop around Littlebury.

Littlebury Church in the nineteenth century (J.M. Youngman)

In prehistoric times there was a ring hill fort at Littlebury, hence the name 'Lytlanbyrig' which means little fort. By Saxon times it belonged to a monastery at Ely. In the seventeenth century Littlebury's great claim to fame was an eccentric resident, Henry Winstanley who built a strange house here, full of practical jokes such as a chair which grasped its occupant and wouldn't let go. The inventor, who was born in Saffron Walden and died in his own lighthouse at Eddystone in 1703, lived near Holy Trinity Church. Here in the peaceful churchyard lie others of note, members of the manorial family, their memorial grander, but their resting place no different from everyman.

Returning to North End, up the hill to the junction, there is a fine view back over Littlebury in its sheltering valley. The weary could catch a bus back to town(normally two-hourly but telephone 01223-423554 for times); or it is possible to take the footpath almost opposite the junction which goes past Westley Farm and so back by the earlier route.

28

But the best way is to turn right ⟹ along the pavement for a pleasant mile past walled Spring Wood along a route used by Bronze Age peoples some three or four thousand years ago. Old maps show a lane crossing Windmill Hill to join another lost road at Duck Street. Spring Wood is not ancient, but was there in the eighteenth century as a plantation. There is a reference in the town archives to a new footpath and a new wall here in 1821.

When the house on the left, The Vineyard, was built in the 1860s, there was an interesting find three feet down, a finely-worked flint knife of Neolithic age, now in the town museum. The Corporation windmill was probably on this side of the road, possibly opposite the top end of the allotments, presumably on what is now a golf course. The mill was granted by charter to the Guild of Holy Trinity in the early sixteenth century, but had gone by the late eighteenth century. Only a name remains, Windmill Hill, the final descent into town past tree-topped flint walls and in spring banks of daffodils.

There are seats provided, looking down on the road deep below. It is interesting to reflect how the landscape might look had one or other of the canal schemes, proposed in late eighteenth and early nineteenth centuries, gone ahead. One scheme would have brought a canal through a tunnel under Windmill Hill by Spring Wood.

The road runs deep below the pavement, partly through thousands of years of use, for this is a prehistoric route; but mainly because it was lowered artificially in 1824 to make the steep run into town safer – until then 'those were bad days for loaded teams', remembered John Player, 'it was a matter of awe as they descended almost unrestrainable, till they reached the town'. This was a job creation scheme, all done with pick and shovel, by otherwise unemployed men who received a shilling or so per day. Documents in the town archives are very revealing of the attitudes which lay behind the apparent worthiness of these schemes, which were really attempts to reduce the escalating poor rates, and to occupy the 'idle poor'.

The class attitudes of the town elite in those days were ingrained: in August 1843 John Player walked back this way and exclaimed: 'We cannot but look with delight at the fields, now crowned with luxuriant corn... the busy reapers will be fully employed, and every class will have an interest in husbanding the grain.' Earlier attempts to grow wheat on the Windmill Hill fields had been a failure for the soil was too light and it yielded badly.

The house-name Vineyard, suggests that grapes grew well on these warm south-facing slopes, and obviously they were also suitable for saffron which made Walden famous and must have been a glorious, albeit short-lived, sight in autumn when the little fields turned purple with the blooms of saffron! The 'crokers', who lived nearby in the little cottages at Bridge End, laboured intensively in small saffron crocus gardens, collecting 30,000 flowers to produce enough stigmas for just one pound of the golden spice, worth more than gold.

The saffron industry was in its heyday from 1400 till 1700, during the course of which Chepyng Walden changed its name – and the rest is history. At the bottom of Windmill Hill, turn right ⇒ along New Pond Lane to return to Swan Meadow: Saffron Walden has thankfully never grown beyond this ancient boundary, and it still forms a rural approach, the familiar church spire rising above the old town.

Coming down Windmill Hill to Bridge End

4 Pounces: 4 miles

Much of Saffron Walden's commerce and industry has tended to concentrate on the east side of town, where the clock tower of Tesco, built on part of Shire Hill Farm, has become a new landmark. This important area for the local economy still adjoins splendid countryside, however, and this short walk, through land once attached to the old sub-manor of Pounces, is full of interest.

Walkers arriving by car can, by courtesy of the management, park in the bottom end of the Tesco store car-park. Turn left ⇐ across the road, then right ⇒ up Elizabeth Way, named after the present queen. In contrast to new development stands the grey old Union Workhouse, still looking more a prison than the 'spacious and airy building' described in the 1840s. The workhouse was there to punish poverty and reduce poor rates: 'the habits of the poor are decidedly improved and their manners become more respectful', it was concluded. But poverty persisted – in the harsh winter of 1895, 11,000 food tickets had to be given to the poor. Used by tramps, it later became known as 'the grubbies'. No one ever seems quite sure what to do with these old workhouses and in 1996 it was up for sale. Perhaps it should join the tourist trail, a memorial to the poor, that is the majority of the population, on whose backs the middle-class prosperity of Saffron Walden was built.

The old Union Workhouse

Turn right ⇒ along the Ashdon road, in past centuries called Whitestreete, presumably due to the chalky soil, and possibly with a Roman connection in the word 'straet' – a silver Roman coin was once found in this area. In the last century this part of town had some particularly appalling slums, Copthall Buildings put up in 1822 to accommodate workers in the short-lived silk weaving industry. This came to an end, and in 1887 so did the rackety homes of the poor, for 17 families were made homeless when a spectacular fire caused by chimney soot gutted the whole lot. One 80-year-old lost all he had.

De Vigier Avenue is named after the owner of Acrows, not long ago a large local employer, which built houses here for workers. Nearby is the spot where many Walden townsfolk took their first flight in 1927 when an Avro pilot landed here. Ex-aviators, known as barnstormers since they slept rough, bought up surplus training aircraft and earned a living giving rides. Leave town on a high-banked footway, and try to ignore the litter – in spring there are white violets and always fine views across the fields. When Acrows(on the site to the left, now Ridgeons) was being put up in 1973, the builders found geological treasure, a huge glacial erratic boulder, at least seven feet wide and 150 million years old. The immense force of ice had carried this huge lump of rock, weighing three tons, hundreds of miles half-a-million years ago to end its days here – or rather outside Saffron Walden Museum, where it now sits.

Ice Age erratic boulder outside Saffron Walden Museum

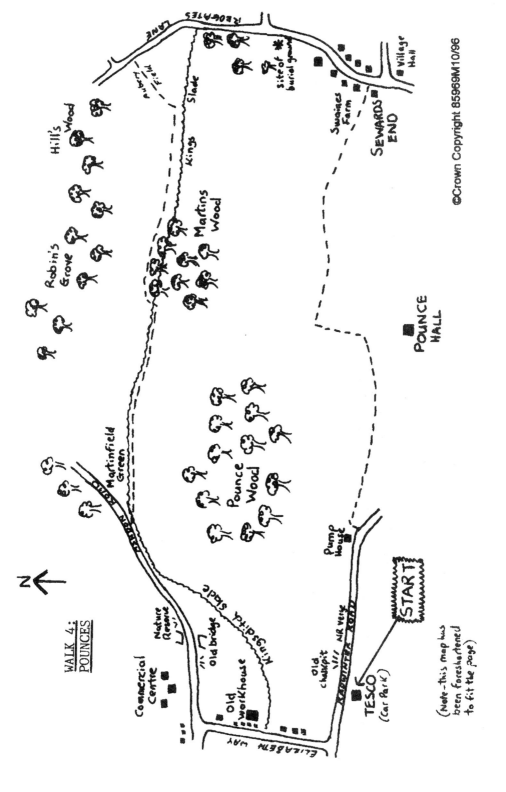

WALK 4:
POUNCES

©Crown Copyright 85969M10/96

(Note - this map has been foreshortened to fit the page)

Unfortunately the footpath ends here, so cross the road and TAKE GREAT CARE! Unfortunately it is not at all safe to linger by the old railway bridge and enjoy the Special Verges, managed by Saffron Walden Town Council for the Highway Authority, specially to conserve the flowers. In this dangerous cutting the soil conditions encourage in turn Milkwort, Rock Rose, Narrow-leaved Everlasting Pea, Crested Cow Wheat and Pepper Saxifrage. Past the bridge, on the other side, Kidney Vetch might be found in wetter seasons in abundance on a raised bank, one of the very few areas where pure chalk emerges from the boulder clay. There are dozens of other species, a microcosm of chalk countryside in just a few yards. And with the flowers come the butterflies, bees and grasshoppers, sheltered by chalk-loving shrubs like spindle and wayfaring tree, the season ending with a glorious harvest of hips and haws, nuts and berries to feed wildlife through the winter.

Hidden above the verge, going back to nature, are the remnants of Acrow Halt, a little platform specially built for the nearby workers. It was a sad day for the town when the line closed in the 1960s, after serving the area for almost a century. This section had been partially built on a track called Grope Court Lane, thought to be the road to St. Aylotts in earlier times. This suggests that, after closure, it could and should have been conserved as a right-of-way – or it would have made a useful off-road cycle-way from Walden to Ashdon.

Ashdon Road Railway Bridge

Martinfield Green and Pounce Wood

The fenced-off enclosure here was first established in 1939 to store high-octane fuel for transporting by rail to local airfields in the War. Attempts were made to bomb it – fortunately unsuccessful, for the town would surely have been blown up too! Continue on the floral verge until the road veers left at Martinfield Green and here turn right ⇒ along a signposted farm track past a sign saying 'Walkers Welcome'. In summer a big clump of Tansy reminds of a useful herb. The dry Slade winds hidden among dense hedging, beneath which patches of Bluebells speak of former ancient woodland – and such is Pounce Wood, the dark shape on the skyline, ancient though partly coniferised, and unlikely now to be 'abundant' with Early Purple and Butterfly Orchids as recorded a century ago.

The local woodlands are still important game reserves, as in times past. Being so near to town, Pounce Wood was a favourite target of nineteenth century poaching gangs, taking pheasants, hares and rabbits – and wood itself in a hard winter: in 1815 someone was fined six shillings, a huge sum, for stealing fuel from Pounce Wood, for the system was for the poor to buy manorial firewood from the chapman, while the rest of the underwood went to feed the maltings of Walden. It is easy to romanticise poaching, but it could be a desperate business – in 1851 a poacher was transported for seven years, after shooting a gamekeeper in Pounce Wood.

This path, following the Slade has been a boundary at least since the sixteenth century, when it may have marked the edge of a sub-manor. In Tudor times there were sheepwalks around here; but the word 'shott' in some of the field-names is also a remnant of open field cultivation. Going back still further, some concentrations of Roman pottery have been found around Pounce Wood, suggesting the fields were in cultivation up to 2,000 years ago. Ahead is Martins

Wood, which seems to be a corruption of Mattens, one of the medieval sub-manors, named after John de Matan of 1248. At one time it belonged to Walden Abbey, and even had its own court, but this sub-manor, one of seven in Walden, was short-lived and joined up with Pounces in Tudor times. Stay on the track to the left of the entrance a few more yards, then turn right ⇒ on 'the path less travelled by', uphill beside ditched and banked ancient woodland, carpeted in Bluebells. The sounds of the wild are all the sounds there are, birdsong and breezes, the squawk of pheasants, the squeaks of two-score of young partridges feeding on the stubble – one partial albino among them. Footprints give away rabbits, foxes and deer; chewed hazelnuts show squirrels at work. Robins Grove stretches away on the horizon. Trees have this noise-absorbing benefit, so still, so peaceful, that town could be a million miles away instead of just down the track.

As Martins Wood thins out into Martyns Grove and hedgerows, look for a gap with a rather misleading waymark post, through the hedge to the right ⇒ over a dry ditch into a meadow where the right-of-way, formerly called Ashden Lane, can be followed diagonally via the overhead wires. This skylark-haunted meadow, dotted with yellow flowers and flowering grasses waving in the breeze, was earlier called Auberie field. If this translates as 'old bury' from the Saxon word *burh*, there may be some manorial connection – the site of a manor-house perhaps? The path emerges through a gap onto Redgates Lane beside an old metal footpath sign of a type now sadly disappearing, but usefully announcing the ways to Saffron Walden and Ashdon. It would be a good idea for local councils to restore these informative and attractive signs.

Aubery Field

Turn right ⇒ along Redgates Lane, the epitome of the English country lane, hedged, quiet, shady, meandering. If, as here, the boundaries on either side alternate, it demonstrates that the lane is older than the field system which, if true, makes it a very old lane indeed. A fine view westwards, somewhat marred by unscreened commerce, encompasses Littlebury Green, Strethall and Arkesden. This lane is a great place for blackberries! And for the bright red berries of wayfaring tree, sallow in damper spots, old ash trees, useful crab apples, and dogwood, sign of an old hedge. In abundance in summer are little Angels' Eyes, Germander Speedwell, blue as the sky. Warblers play treble in treetops while cuckoo plays bass in distant woods. A plus for Walden is that one of the latest recorded dates of 'cuckoo-cuckoo' was in the parish on 12th October 1957.

Somewhere along is a point 384 feet above sea level, near where the King's Slade begins its journey to Saffron Walden Common and thence the Granta. Old Noake, who farmed hereabouts in medieval times, must have got his water from the Slade: now Nokes, seen through a gap to the right, is reverting to scrub, perfect hunting ground for kestrels. Around New House Lane – formerly Wills Ayly, before that Pappeslane – was Kelkesgreene named from a fourteenth century family. The casual walker would never guess that on the right almost opposite this lane lies an old graveyard, said to date from very early times, later known as a dissenters' burial ground.

The countryside ends beside an old farm still lived in but seemingly frozen in time, hidden behind piles of outdated forgotten things, ancient Sunbeam Rapiers incongruously alongside wooden haycarts and a Chalmers caterpillar tractor, all festooned in rampant undergrowth, birds and mice nesting in the rusty cavities. It would be a shame to tidy it up, this treasure trove of ancient bits and bobs from another age. A pond full of bulrushes, glimpsed through the hedge, may be part of a medieval moat system, reputedly to keep out the Plague. The flint wall contains pieces of blue Kentish ragstone, brought here in medieval times when the River Pant was allegedly navigable up to Radwinter.

Round the bend lies a cluster of houses old and new. Go past the camp-site and turn right ⇒ at a concrete footpath sign, over a tall stile and along a gravelled path beside stables to the next gate. Take a narrow rutted track between an electrified fence and hedge, and through another gate, being careful to close it. A fence and plank bridge then lead into a long narrow field, once called Swaines – Richard de Sweyn was granted the land in the fourteenth century, but its history goes back much further.

From here on, the paths run through arable fields and are not always easy to walk on. In the long narrow field, head for a small gap twenty yards to the left of a large one, through which there is a wonderful view of Walden spread out below, for Sewards End is so much higher than the town. This field was once Littlea, suggesting old meadowland, and the path was a grass balk until recently – if it is unclear, use the ever-present church spire as a guide! An old humpy meadow is seen across a stile, full of lambs in spring(keep dogs on leads). It is so rare to see sheep in Walden countryside, where once they were everywhere. The recommended route is round the outside hedge of this meadow, turning left and right, a pleasant downhill walk with fine views, on soft loamy soil past old pond and tumbled hedgebanks of blackberry and sloe. The old name here, Kitchen Field, suggests it grew vegetables for kitchen use at Pounces. At various points are glimpses of this house,' agreeably and prominently situated' as described 150 years ago. It was built in the early seventeenth century on the same site as the original wooden hall erected by Siward, after whom Sewards End is named, 600 years earlier. He, however, preferred to live in town. Nor did Siward's grandson Albold Pouncyn, who received 'totam terram Siwardi avi sui' in the twelfth century, bother to live here much – it is odd how immortality has been attained by men who contributed less than others who did so much and are forgotten – land is the reason. However, a later Pouncyn was a witness to a Walden Charter in 1300, so they were obviously still important.

Turn left ⇐ down a short track and right ⇒ along an elevated footway towards the town, passing the overgrown concrete pump house constructed in 1905 to pump water twice a day, from the town up the hill to the then-new Sewards End water tower – to the tune of 5,600 gallons a day. In 1967 the old system was replaced with automatic pumping.

Once again there are flowers to enjoy, for the high bank supports Cowslips and an interesting chalk flora of Salad Burnet, Scabious, Restharrow and delicate little Harebells. The interesting wild flowers of Walden owe much to the underlying chalk, seen in its thickness in the old quarry. Exposed chalk can be as much as 150 metres thick in Saffron Walden, all composed of the remains of sea creatures from a shallow sea which covered England 80 million years ago. Something to ponder on, while stirring a nice cuppa in the Tesco coffee shop!

Old tractor at Sewards End

5 Thunderley: 5 miles

Much of Saffron Walden's development between the wars was on the south side of town where the names Pleasant Valley and Landscape View are reminders of what a Victorian writer called the 'joyous view for many miles', still visible from the top of the Debden Road water tower, built 87 feet high in 1913 to supply new homes. But people have to live somewhere, and these are attractive estates. Moreover residents of the Fairview Estate are lucky to have easy footpath access to the pleasant valley of the Fulfen Slade and the lost parish of Thunderley.

*Debden Road
Water Tower*

Begin the walk in the middle of the housing estate, in Ross Close, at the primary school named after Katherine Semar, a Tudor benefactress of the town. To the right of the school, follow a concrete signpost past houses and flats, and the school's wildlife area. Keep beside the fence, then cross diagonally to the left over Herberts Farm Playing Field, heading for the larger of two gaps in the hedge A half-hidden waymark post points ahead along a farm road beside neat maple hedge to Herberts, an attractive house built in the 1600s with weathervane, pargetting, sixteenth-century flint-walled, timber-framed barn and, in summer, some glorious roses. The name, as often happens, is much older than the house,

39

traceable to John Herberd of 1269. Did he originally clear the trees to build a long-ago cottage? Medieval field names like Redding, 'cleared land' and Stocking, 'tree stumps' reflect this process. Herberts flourished, reaching the status of yeoman's farm by the seventeenth-century, set amidst an area of open fields. Land hereabouts was good for barley, reflected in a medieval field-name Bygstaple.

Opposite Herberts turn right ⇒ along a waymarked grass track, good for blackberrying in autumn, then left ⇐ following a deep ditch, full of common 'weeds', all with a herbal use to country people in the past: Ground Ivy used to make gill ale; Forget-me-not once thought to cure lung problems; Yarrow used by Anglo-Saxons to heal wounds; Broad-leaved Willowherb recommended by Culpeper for bleeding; and Wild Teasel whose cultivated cousins are still used to raise the nap of woollen cloth. Around here are the fields where, sixty years ago there was huge excitement because the two-day Essex Show came to Saffron Walden, with 25,000 people arriving for farming, horticultural and historical events – in later times this must have seemed to belong to some halcyon pre-war idyll.

Turn right ⇒ to pass a stand of eight fine oaks, flourishing on the orange-brown boulder clay, offering habitat to a myriad species, from caterpillars to oak galls. Herberds was established, as settlements often were, right on the boundary between this glacial drift, remnant of the ice age, and the chalk, remnant of primeval sea creatures. This is a good walk for wild flowers – newly-scoured ditches splashed with Field Poppies whose seeds can lie dormant for a century awaiting this opportunity; yellow Perforate St John's Wort, enjoying the chalkier patches; and Red Campion in rich soil.

These windswept open fields offer wide views, as the path dips toward a more intimate landscape, the valley of The Roos, a sixteenth century farmhouse on an older site – how well early farmers chose their sheltered havens. A Victorian naturalist who lived there, Joshua Clarke, would have known the Wild Basil, Meadow Vetchling and Field Scabious which survive today. But we have lost many of the 28 plants for which in 1851 he won a prestigious award for rare flowering native plants, all of them *picked* from round Walden – they included the Maiden Pink and Fragrant Orchid. More remarkable, perhaps, is that some of his bunch, like Crested Cow Wheat and Sulphur Clover *have* survived around the parish. The Roos, a pre-Domesday farm site, part of Audley End estates and still a working farm a thousand years on, owes its name to Gilbert de Ros of 1254. Beyond 400-year-old barns and stables were fields called Dovehouse closes and Coney grene, reminders of medieval times, when doves and rabbits were not only an important source of meat, but also owning cotes and warrens was a kind of status symbol for the better-off landowners. Rabbits, then rather delicate creatures needing special care, have adapted to changing circumstances!

Turn left along a signposted byway, an ancient lane, medieval or older, being once part of the road from Thaxted through what is now Beechy Ride to the old Abbey. Nothing in the countryside is more special than these old green ways, of which Essex has about 500 miles, plus another 4,000 miles of footpaths and

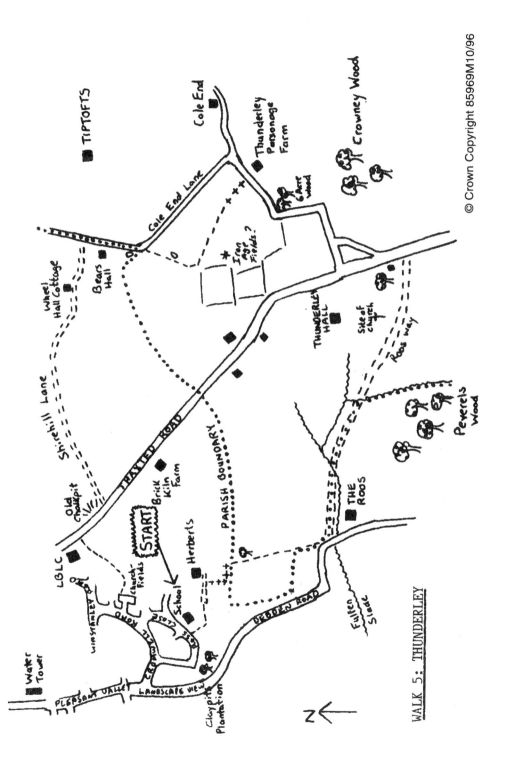

WALK 5: THUNDERLEY

© Crown Copyright 85969M10/96

bridleways. In spring 1843, the Victorian writer, John Player waxed lyrical about this 'broad green lane, verdant as ever' where travellers, 'the wandering tribe may find a spot to pitch their tent, and suspend the kettle above the freeman's hearth'. Tramps were ever thus tolerated down the lanes, but not in town where magistrates might whip them on their way.

The old lane runs beside an often dry Fulfen Slade, a thick-hedged, mossy way, of dappled glade, brambly hollow and tumbled woodland, sometimes meeting overhead in 'a tunnel of green gloom'; of birdsong – tits, finches and warblers; of butterflies – tortoiseshells, commas, browns feasting on thistle-heads, bramble flowers, weedy pink bindweed; of secretive creatures, fox and deer, leaving only footprints in the ford. On a still, hot day, the buzz of bees is all the sound there is; in autumn the leaves lie thick, absorbing sound: 'And quiet did quiet remain'. Such precious places should remain inviolate, unpolluted, unvehicled. And yet, we live in better times: a water tower, across country to the left, reminds of a time when clean water was not a birthright; an old pillbox, through a gap to the right on army training land, reflects how real was the threat of invasion only half-a-century ago.

The parish boundary follows the Roos way for a bit, then goes up right to Peverel's Wood, where it also forms an important estate boundary with Debden Hall, owned in the twelfth century by William Peverell. But Peverell lost everything when he had to flee the country after poisoning the Earl of Chester in 1153. Another gap gives view of Thunderley Hall – in 1293 Edward I granted Walden Abbey 'free warren' at Thunderley, which refers to hunting as well as rabbit-farming. Perhaps John de Tonderle, a witness to the 1300 Walden charter, took his surname from Thunderley, not vice versa, as the name is much older, a link with Thor, a god of pagan England. Its earliest form, Tunresleam in 1086, translates as 'Thunor's clearing'. Until 1425 this was a separate parish with three manors, but then was joined to Wimbish. Nothing now remains of its little church, ploughed over in the field to the left during the War, nor its churchyard near the main road.

The busy main road is a later bypass, the original Walden road being the lane opposite – cross over to this peaceful little lane, dotted with fine trees of ash and maple and horse chestnut, and floral verges of yellow Lady's Bedstraw, white Meadowsweet, blue Scabious and the purple climbing Tufted Vetch. It is good to hear the yellowhammers' 'little-bit-of-bread-and-no-cheese' song in several places on this walk, as these beautiful summer visitors have declined by over ten per cent in recent years – hedges and woods are so vital to birdlife. Crowney Wood, seen in the distance, was once known for hunting and for its excellent thatching stakes.

There are some interesting field-names along Cole End Lane. One called Schoolings once had a cottage, suggesting some education connection. The old names of the fields ahead from the T-junction were Wither, Middle and Farther Fair Ley, but this does not mean fine field, being a corruption of 'Fouley' denoting the opposite, actually 'filthy clearing'! If this was a medieval field-name, it may have been secondary clearance because there is something else here: on old maps, and still today, the fields have unusually straight edges, which are said to be survivals of an Iron Age rectilinear grid pattern, quite unlike the normal sinuous field boundaries of ancient countryside. The sharp bends of this lane seem to fit the pattern. These fields may thus have been in almost continuous cultivation for about 2,500 years. There is only topographical observation, not archaeological evidence, but what is unusual is not the notion that Iron Age man was perfectly capable of farming efficiently, but that any evidence of prehistoric agriculture should survive on the ground.

Turn right ⟹ at this T-junction, veering left past Six-Acre Wood to pass the beautifully-tended garden of 'swallow-thronged' Thunderley Parsonage Farm, a lovely old house, once part of the glebelands, so the Wimbish Tithe Barn was here. Thousands of trees have been planted on local land – an act of altruism, particularly with oaks which far outlive our own span. But then those who create, and those who destroy, often seem to inhabit different planets.

Thunderley Parsonage Farm

43

The farm is part of Cole End, a tiny settlement possibly originally a woodland charcoal-burning area. It is all very peaceful, but has not always been so. A local tale speaks of a Vicar who in 1879 refused to bury a man who was killed at Cole End Farm, because he had not been baptised. There was drama, too, during the Battle of Britain when a huge formation of German Dornier aircraft mounted an attack on Debden airfield in August 1940. One Dornier engaged by Hurricanes came down somewhere round Cole End – the four German aircrew baled out and were taken prisoner.

Turn left ⇐ opposite the farm along a good grass track lined with tall hedgerows, poplars interspersed with oaks, and footed with Cowslips in spring. Reaching a small plantation, turn right ⇒ to follow a maple and oak hedge past a pond and back to Cole End Lane. Here is another pond, somewhat hidden, which seems likely to have been a parish boundary marker in the days of beating the bounds, since the boundary changes direction here to follow the road. The parish boundary hedges are unusually rich in species with oak, ash, maple, hazel, dogwood, willow, sloe, hawthorn and, a sign of old woodland, clambering wild honeysuckle.

Turn left ⇐ and down the road is Bears Hall first recorded as Beares in 1514 – the origin of the name is uncertain: the Saxon word *baer* refers to swine which fed on pannage of acorns, but there was also a man named Beare who owned land hereabouts. The seventeenth century house was built with bricks made from local clay. In spring there are masses of snowdrops.

Across the field can be seen moated Tiptofts, in part 600 years old and a building of rare beauty, which fortunately survived an arson attack in 1851 which caused £3,000 worth of damage to the farm – hundreds of people came to watch, as farm buildings full of crops burned down: such incendiarism was not uncommon then, for they were troubled times when poor labourers had no other means to express despair.

Turn left ⇐ to a signposted bridleway past Wheel Hall Cottage where someone loves roses. This may come from another Saxon name, *weald* so the present cottage may be built on a much earlier site. This track lacks the quieter charms of the Roos way, perhaps through its use earlier this century as a tramway connecting Thaxted Road and Cole End Lane, transporting clay to the cement works, which product was used to build the airfield at Debden in the 1930s. For a while it was actually called Cement Works Lane – not very romantic! In 1605 it was Sherehil lane, although not apparently named from the Thomas Upsheyre who farmed ten acres six centuries ago. Various old maps call it Tiptoftwaye or Arches Lane, but now it is Shirehill Lane again.

The track is poorly drained, encouraging Pendulous Sedge and osier willow. But this deeply-banked hollow way is soothing, nonetheless, through butterfly-haunted glade and shady tall hedgerow meeting overhead. Dead trees are left to decay with dignity, robins and brimstone butterflies are aloft, amid patches of wild Comfrey, Herb Robert, Burdock and Mugwort. A high bank, the site of an old claypit, is good for blackberrying, decorated with the climbing purple Tufted Vetch. The field opposite to the right of here was Draisland, three pightles and groves which used to belong to the Guild of our Ladie of Pitty in Walden, and later was a charitable bequest left to provide money for 'amendynge the foule highwaies' around Sewards End in the 1480s – almost 400 years later, the Victorian writer John Player noted that the main road to Sewards End was still not much better.

Roads have always been controversial, the more so in an age when Saffron Walden, like all towns, is becoming clogged with traffic. As long ago as 1938 there were radical proposals to bypass the town, and the favoured route for the south side would have dramatically altered all the countryside we still enjoy today. From this lane, for instance, there might now be a view of dual carriageway across to the right, albeit screened with extra development. It may still happen – make the most of these peaceful walks while you still can!

Overgrown meadow-land encourages wildlife, as the old way becomes a gentle grassy path back to town, footed in spring with masses of white and purple Violets. In spring, too, clouds of lemon yellow pussy-willow catkins light up the damp wood across the field, offering valuable early nectar for bees, hover-flies and moths – rather cleverly, male sallow trees make sucrose nectar, and the females make glucose. Sallow was one of the first trees to establish 12,000 years ago when the ice age ended, which is perhaps why it has had time to be exploited by 266 different insects.

Shirehill Lane is one of the few paths where litter can be noticeable, when the disguise of summer vegetation has died away. Some bright spark once estimated that discarded bottles and cans kill at least 100,000 shrews and voles a year in Essex – they get in, but they can't get out. Chalk is near the surface here – it shows in ditches full of wildflowers, and in the flourishing of Old Man's Beard, the wild clematis; and the path emerges beside an old quarry, perhaps the same one complained of in Walden Quarter Sessions in the last century, because the diggings were undermining the narrow Thaxted road. During the last War this disused chalkpit was used by RAF Debden as an ops. room. Here too are the remains of a limekiln. Some say the Romans dug chalk here.

Up the road to the left, opposite Brick Kiln Farm, was 'Ben Hull's Grave', the legendary burial place of a suicide victim, buried at night: John Player, described in lurid terms 'the unceremonious entombment, attended by the appalling stake, driven through the wretched remains.' This is out of the way, however – instead turn right ⇒ and cross the busy road. Opposite where the pavement begins, turn left ⇐ through a rather hidden gate into the playing fields beside the Lord Butler Leisure Centre. This was built near a field where the first aeroplane to land in Walden caused great excitement in 1912. Opened in 1984, the Centre was named after the late 'Rab' Butler, local MP for 36 years, holder of many important government positions and often described as 'the greatest prime minister we never had'.

Walk up the grass playing field straight to the top right-hand corner, to return to the Fairview Estate. Turn left ⇐ then right into Churchfields, left ⇐ to Cromwell Road and left ⇐ again to return to Ross Close.

Saffron Walden is conscientious about celebrating its past and, as well as commemorating the great Lord Butler, the street-names on the estate often are a history lesson in themselves, echoing former personalities or old fields. Nearby is Winstanley Road after a noted Walden family, of whom one member was the extraordinary eccentric engineer, Henry Winstanley who perished in his own Eddystone Lighthouse in 1703. Cromwell Road recalls that general's visit to the town during the Civil War in 1647, when important debates on democracy took place in the Saffron Walden Parish Church; and Ross Close links with the fourteenth century de Ros family of The Roos, whose pleasant valley landscape view has been traversed on this fascinating walk.

The Roos

46

6 Beechy Ride: 5 miles

In many ways Saffron Walden feels more like a big village than a town, for nowhere is it far from the countryside, and after all most of the built-up areas were fields earlier this century. The opposite process has occurred at Audley End Village, originally known as Brookwalden which was a substantial community in medieval times, but has dwindled to a one-street hamlet. It is all the more attractive for that, a rather special little place, often unnoticed beside its more famous namesake. Here is a peaceful spot to picnic beneath pine and lime, oak and horse chestnut, before exploring the medieval road to Roos and the valley of the Fulfen.

Brocwalden, as spelt in 1400, had over 50 houses in three streets, one of which was an important road along the River Cam. Almost the only remnant of this lost road is the one here now, once called Osiers Lane. Sited where the Fulfen Slade met the Cam, the hamlet was built specially to house workers at Walden Abbey and was a self-contained community. Perhaps that was why there was 'a great mortality' in 1365, taking off most of the Abbey servants and tenants.

Medieval names – Monksmell and Fullynmell – suggest there were watermills nearby, used for grinding corn and fulling cloth, and the Tuesday market, granted by 1295, was held in the High Street, now Audley End Road, where there were terraced houses. After the Abbey closed, it was still well-populated for a period, and later a planned village was erected in Osiers Lane.

Even in the last century, it was still a busy little place, with grocer, shoemaker, beerhouse and a school with up to 60 children, now the post office, beside which is a pre-war, cast-iron red telephone box, now a listed historic monument. So too are the cottages, numbers 2-20 being the oldest. Some coins and old pottery have been found hereabouts.

Go along the lane past an old pump opposite which a large buddleia offers nectar for a score of aristocrat butterflies – 1996 was the best year ever for painted ladies, which find their way here from Africa. Under a little footbridge, the Fulfen Slade trickles, reflecting blue sky and rippled trees, including over the wall on the right one huge magnificent oak.

This is by the entrance to the College of St Mark – here turn left ⇐ through a waymarked gate unfortunately marked 'private'. In winter, when the trees are bare, the lovely old building, with a cross on the roof, can be glimpsed through an old gate. Grade-one listed and therefore special even by Saffron Walden standards, it was originally a small hospital built for the Abbey peasants, reputedly named from St Mark's Day 1258 when it was consecrated. Before gas pipes were laid in the early 1990s, archaeologists found the foundations of the hospital, which had fallen into decay when the Abbey closed – centuries later during an agricultural phase it was still known as Hospital Farm.

In the early 1600s the medieval plan of the old *infirmaria* was followed in its rebuilding as almshouses, with wings round two courtyards and a chapel.

Renovated a fourth time about 50 years ago as a home for retired clergy, this spot is now enjoying its fifth reincarnation as a church centre for young people – their recreation area can be seen in the seventeenth century walled garden. It is hard to imagine a lovelier place to stay – or to walk, past mellow old brick wall, grey willow and tall pink Willowherb to the music of songbirds.

The College of St. Mark

Continue down the track past the modern farmyard, now called Donrobin, beside which the few modern houses have an enviable view of open woodland dotted in winter with naturalised snowdrops. The springs in Fulvanmeade explain its Tudor name, wet meadow, and such damp streamside offers perfect site for the whispering aspen, *populus tremula*: 'the aspen heaves its rainy-sounding silver leaves'. At the end of the track, in a sunny glade in late summer, there is evidence of how flowering thistles make immeasurable contributions to the invertebrate population: buzzing and flitting and feeding are a multitude of meadow browns, tortoiseshells, whites, red admirals, painted ladies, bumble bees, ladybirds, flies, moths, grasshoppers and all kinds of bugs.

48

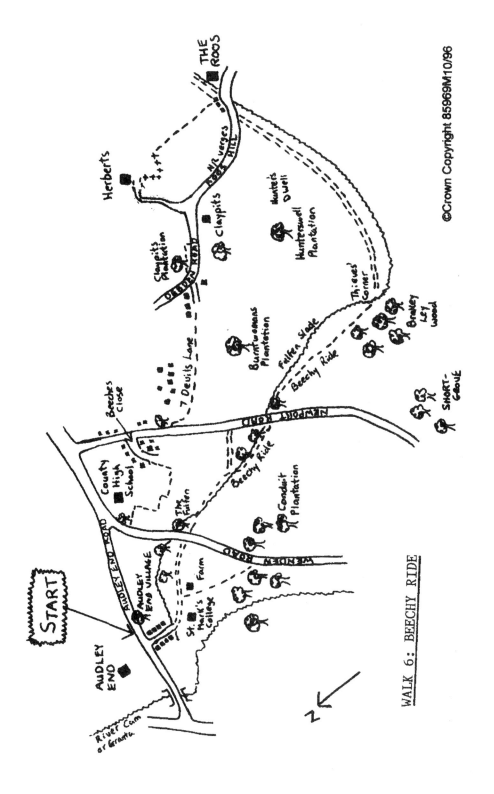

WALK 6: BEECHY RIDE

©Crown Copyright 85969M10/96

Stand a few seconds and listen, on a day of high summer, just before harvest, and hear 'all the live murmur of a summer's day', the buzzing bees, the whispering aspen, the crack of ripening wheat, and it is extraordinary how sound and smell, rather than sight, have the power to transfix a moment out of time. Then someone whizzes by in a car, and the moment is gone.

Wheat field near Donrobin Farm

Cross the Wenden Road and turn left ⇐ along the pavement, over a footbridge of the Fulfen Slade, after which the road is sunken below a tall hedgebank. Turn right ⇒ at a rather hidden signpost along the County High School fence beside an old hedgerow which reflects the chalky soil with its maple, spindle and hazel, and the hard-to-spot plants of Milk Vetch. There are extensive views right across the wooded valley and hills, with the windsock and hangar of a private airstrip in the distance – such splendid countryside, yet so near the town. Deep beneath the school field, this path appears to be the original line of an important medieval 'king's highway' which ran from the Abbey to Debden, but declined after the Dissolution. This ancient road can still be followed but a planned extension of the school playing field may entail diversion. The secondary school was first built in the 1950s, on land bought by compulsory purchase. An old field name hereabouts was Maypole Close, possibly connected with these semi-pagan festivities, but if so it is not documented.

Within the fence the playing field occupies not only part of the medieval road, but also a section of the now defunct railway. Looking across, it is almost impossible to see where the railway crossed the valley for, after it closed in 1964, Audley End Estates filled in the 45-feet high cutting, and restored the contours just as they were when the railway was built – so you would never know it had chuffed this way for almost 100 years. Building it in the first place had been a hugely costly exercise entailing the manual moving of 65,000 tons of earth in this area. The first turf was cut quite near here on 18th May 1863 but someone forgot the spade! The churches became concerned about the rough Irish navvies who built the railway, and organised open-air mass for them down below under the beech trees, and even employed someone specifically to mission the railway workers. There were several mishaps in the Beechy Ride cutting: in 1873 a connecting rod broke and the passengers had to walk to Audley End; in 1902 a train collided with some wagons, rolling out of control down the cutting in the dark, but again no one was injured – they all just got out and walked to the station; and during the last War a Luftwaffe fighter shot up a train here.

In the old railway cutting the school Farm Club sometimes keeps its small flock of sheep, a nice touch for this may have been part of the Abbey Infold, where the ewes were pastured, while the wethers, kept for wool, lived on the more distant Outfold. Sheep are now sadly scarce in Walden fields, where once 'the sound of sheep unshepherded, the sound of sheep in fold' was a commonplace, for the monks kept thousands. Perhaps scholastic and monastic sheep graze the same lands on Sheepcoat Hill! The medieval or even Saxon name was Settecuppe, a field-name commonly attached to isolated, rounded hills in Essex, meaning flat-topped hill.

Follow the fenced path till it comes out behind houses, to emerge beside a black plastic footpath sign at Beeches Close, a residential road with many attractive gardens. On the corner at the junction with the main road there remains a small 'T and C' marker post, remnant of differential town/country rating systems. Turn right ⇒ a few yards along the green with its lovely trees, and cross the road left ⇐ to climb a signposted but overgrown footpath opposite. From a grassy area at the top there is a surprisingly steep drop to the Newport road below, and the achievement of labourers in 1826, digging this cutting with just pick and shovel through the chalk hillside, can be appreciated. Although they got a shilling or so a day, and it was a job creation scheme, it also reduced poor rates, and the 'idle poor' if they refused could be prosecuted at Sessions. It was a scheme won therefore with men's sweat but actually quite useful since until then mail coaches had struggled up this and other local hills with great difficulty. One incidental benefit of their labours was that the exposed cutting offered habitat to chalkland flora, but the banks are now overgrown and in any case much too dangerous to go flower-watching.

At the top is a sort of village green, thoughtfully retained along the back of this whole estate, which enables walkers to still tread the old Seven Devils Lane, a continuation of the road from Audley End over Sedcop Hill which would here have formed a cross-roads with the Newport road, known at this point as Gallows Hill after nearby fields of the same name. The parish accounts do contain a few entries such as, in 1631, 4s.4d. 'payd for tymber, and making the gallowes', but there is no documentation to prove that this was a place of execution, nor that Seven Devils Lane refers to the ghosts of the gallows. The number seven was always significant in folklore, and it may have been difficult land to cultivate – we still use 'devil' in this sense.

This is certainly the place for creepy field-names, though. The field to the right was Burndwomans shott – clearly some association with fire in the distant past, referred to also in Blackeland shotte, but there is no evidence of witch-burning. The older name was Brende melleshott, recorded in 1400, meaning 'burnt mill'. Without documentary proof, these field-names are tantalising. Go to the far edge of the green and turn left ⇐ along a pleasant track, sheltered with overgrown hawthorn trees, much used by the residents. At the end of Seven Devils Lane, turn right ⇒ along the Debden Road for about 100 yards and, opposite a copper beech tree, cross the road onto a track opposite.

Claypits in the Nineteenth Century (J.M. Youngman)

52

After a few yards, turn right ⇒ down a newly restored bark path through Claypits Plantation – 'cleypetes' occur naturally where boulder clay and chalk meet together and were useful for marling the land to increase fertility. Abandoned, this one has become a very pleasant woody nature reserve, maintained by the District Council. Is this perhaps where a Victorian writer, John Player noted 'the nightingale sweetly warbles from his favourite haunt'? Nightingales are very rare in Essex now. Go up the steps to Herberts Farm Playing Field, turn right ⇒ then left ⇐ along the road past Claypits House just past which some walkers may prefer to get off the busy road, taking the Herberts route instead. But it is interesting to look at the Special Verges: while a dangerous cutting supports typical chalk flora, Hoary Plantain, Salad Burnet, Rock Rose and Marjoram, soil changes on the level roadsides encourage different flowers, Lesser Periwinkle and Sulphur Clover. Although managed by Saffron Walden Town Council on behalf of Essex Highways Department, the credit for the conservation of the 48 Special Verges in Uttlesford must go to an indefatigable Saffron Walden botanist, Joan Mummery. Saffron Walden has a tradition of botany, no doubt because of its interesting soils – it was another Walden botanist, George Stacey Gibson who produced the 1862 Flora of Essex, for long the standard reference – five thousand people watched the funeral of this remarkable man; and another one, Joshua Clarke, was associated with The Roos, to which the road continues.

Before that, just before the first redbrick cottage, turn right ⇒ onto a straight path between fields. The Fulfen, which runs parallel to this path, used to run across the road by The Roos. Beside it were pastures and meadows, while up here the land was open field, acre upon acre of common arable, patrolled by skylarks, 'spilling their rubbed and round pebbles of sound in air's still lake'. They seem to be common enough round Walden, and it would be unthinkable for skylarks to go the same way as kites, after which Puttockes field is named – once decimated by gamekeepers.

Up the slope to the left is the parish boundary of Walden, a line marked out over a thousand years ago, and once of crucial importance, in the days before the Ordnance Survey brilliantly got to work, before which the precise location of the bounds had to be passed on in the oral tradition. An interest in wild flowers enlivens every walk in the chalklands – here are Wild Parsnip, Field Scabious, Lady's Bedstraw and Weld along the track. Modern agriculture has made some arable weeds rarities, but fortunately many of them can lie dormant for years until opportunity presents itself. Thus the sloping field to the right some years becomes a colourful, natural garden of pale pink Fumitory and lime-green Sun Spurge, of Red Campion and the multi-coloured faces of little Field Pansies. Near the end of the trees the path veers right ⇒ round Brakey Ley Wood, where yellow catkins catch the sun in early spring. Brakey Ley was pasture land in the eighteenth century, so it is not ancient woodland, yet has a wild beauty, old beeches hiding a rabbit-burrowed, woody slade. Here the path still follows an ancient way from

Walden Abbey to Debden, and also in much more modern times part of the Harcamlow Way, a long-distance route from Harlow to Cambridge. A waymark to the left ⇐ across a dry, stony ford, marks Thieves' Corner, allegedly the haunt of highway robbers in times past, but again popular names can mislead – elsewhere such terms have simply related to poor fertility. But there is at least one recorded crime hereabouts: one day in 1826 the landlord of the Hoops Inn travelling through Puttocks fields was mugged but saved by another man hearing his cries for help. In a sense the countryside, which so many people are too nervous to walk in alone, is now much safer than in the good old days! More law-abiding poor men had a rotten life – picking stones for road repairs was a typical job and in 1838, for instance, the pits near here yielded 1,387 stones, for which the men earned 1s.4d. a day plus beer. An old pit once over to the right had another use – as shooting practice and was known as Butts Corner. Today Thieves' Corner has gone back to nature, with tumbled trees allowed to lie, a habitat as valuable in death as in life, full of fungi and invertebrates, nature's own recycling depot.

Emerging into the open, the correct path is ahead on a bank at the other side of the hedge, which marks the parish boundary. This field-edge gives a view up the hill to the left of Limekiln Plantation at Shortgrove, an ancient estate which became part of the parish of Newport in the twelfth century. The name derives from short ditch, reference to an ancient sunken trackway used by packhorse traffic, before the present road evolved. Shortgrove Hall burnt down in 1966 and was later demolished. It is a long time since walkers were allowed through, since all footpaths on the estate were closed in 1788 so the owner could have privacy, in return for a new bridge over the river at Sparrows Hill.

Through a gap to the right can be seen a nineteenth century plantation on the site of an old pit, still known by its Tudor name, Hunterswell. Nearby have been found worked flints, suggesting that Neolithic man explored these parts. The field on the left once had a small two-acre close with a little bit of rural history attached: it was free by deed so long as its owner paid 'to the Manor of Brookwalden a Red Rose at the Feast of the nativity of St John the Baptist', a form of 'quit rent'

Reaching the trees, turn right and then left through the open glades of high-banked Beechy Ride, still lovely albeit but a shadow of the 'beech tree cathedral' which once formed an avenue across to Audley End. A map of 1788 shows 28 trees on this side of the road, and more than twice as many on the other side. A good age for a beech is 200 years and many are now dead and dying in storms. Yet there is life in death, for many creatures like beetles and centipedes thrive in old stumps, and the gaps allow new saplings to come through, while sunny glades encourage Bluebells, Cowslips and Harebells enjoyed by butterflies and moths who need the nectar, as squirrels, woodmice and birds enjoy the beechmast.

'Beechy Ride'

Here and there are signs of campfires, reminiscent of the old days when 'men of the road' might stop by here to boil up their billycans. In past centuries they might dine on fruit – a medieval field name, Peritonfeild, indicates wild pear trees hereabouts. These old field names are very revealing of so much lost lore about the countryside, but also this part of Walden parish is rather special in that field-names enable a reconstruction of the medieval farming system, for where the slope changed, so did the name and rotation of crops, fallow/winter-sown/spring-sown. The names of the middle ages have a singsong poetry all their own – Werkwey Shott and Goodzenedell, Parva Redyng and Setewenedane.

Go through a blackthorn thicket up to Port Bridge, called Portbrugge in medieval times, meaning entrance to the parish, built over the deep ravine of the Slade. The road nearby at Sparrows End Hill was lowered in the late 1820s, again using the unemployed poor as cheap labour. The Corporation had hoped that, once the roads were improved, more London traffic would come this way, but it never happened and, like the lost canal and the short-lived railway, Walden remained in its backwater, which of course is why it remains such an attractive place today. Cross the road with great care to a signposted path directly opposite, with a good view of the bridge. Go through the thicket, walking above The Fulfen Slade, scrunching along a carpet of beech nut husks, right next to the road, yet in another world: it's nice here, 'a quiet place, that's green, away from all mankind'. It is sad, driving into town past the familiar, well-loved view of leafy slade amid chalky slopes, to see these very old trees disappearing one by one in winter storms, but a natural process and meanwhile, the dead trunks are statuesque in their dying, and hugely valuable for wildlife in their decay. In late winter the last few haws and new catkins attract the birds, a few Violets grow still, offering early nectar. We have lost the chalkland butterflies of pastoral periods, but still on sunny spring days, ephemeral butterflies flit among the glades – brimstones and orange tips and tortoiseshells, beautiful names, beautiful creatures. In his poems of the last century John Player tried to capture this quality: 'I fly the crowded mall For groves of beech; and in secluded vale On sunny morn, I woo the tranquil shade.' He was, perhaps, a better mayor than poet.

The field up to the left once had a curious name, The Whampe, derived perhaps from an Old Norse word, a sign of Scandinavian influence locally. At the end of the trees the path crosses to the other side of the Slade, near where the railway once crossed. It is striking, from this wide chalky track, to compare these big open fields with ancient woody countryside on the other side of town, here the well-drained slopes and there puddled ponds in the clay, here the beech and there the oak.

From Wenden Road it is straight across back to Audley End Village, but there is a pleasant diversion: turn left ⇐ beside floral banks up the road once a green lane variously known as Fulfen, Fulvans, Felfurn or Fieldfare Lane. In 1847 this was widened as it was too narrow for carriages to pass en route to the then-new railway station at Wenden. Lord Braybrooke gave the land on condition that the council allowed him to divert an inconvenient footpath from Audley End to Sir Joshua's Bridge. This is reminiscent of the same ploy used by the owner of Shortgrove Hall a generation before – what we now call 'planning gain', but thereby we have lost many old paths.

Take care of traffic. Just before the wall, turn right ⇒ through a broken kissing-gate, along a track by Conduit Wood, named from the Abbey water-pipe which ran along here. This is a quiet grassy way, dotted with wild flowers, a suntrap beside a cool, dark woodland full of wildlife, its edges offering autumn harvest of hips and haws, sloes and elderberries. Over the wall can be seen water, evidence of many springs, hence its use as Ozier Ground. There is a back view of the College of St Mark, then go through the farmyard and left ⇐ back to the starting point, where in season refreshments can be had from the teashop at the post office.

Audley End Village

St. James' Church

7 Sewards End: 4³/₄ miles

There is more to Sewards End than meets the eye. On the surface it looks an ordinary little hamlet, but history is in plenty, and here on the boulder clay at the head of the Kingsgate valley, there are fine walks in ancient countryside, following in the steps of the Romans, and past places associated with medieval monasticism. Eight or nine centuries on, the names of early farmers and of the great landowners, Siward and Pouncyn, continue in use for house and hamlet. While much has changed – the windmill long gone, the last pub demolished, the shop recently closed – the community is being revitalised with its chapel renamed and a smart new village hall.

A good place to begin the walk is at the new Sewards End Village Hall(who are kindly allowing walkers to park so long as there are no functions in progress). Opened in 1995, it replaced the old Nissen hut opposite, which had come to the end of its days. Opposite is The Old Fox, said to have been a drinking place almost since Tudor times – during the last war it was in use as an air-raid warden post. Turn right here ⟹ along Redgates Lane, full of attractive houses, notably sixteenth century Birbecks of fine chimneys and barns, and the Old Smithy, formerly called Brewery Cottage. Like Swaines Farm, an ancient site perhaps named from the Saxon word for swine, they have remnants of medieval moats reputedly to keep out the Plague. North-west Essex has a great many houses with moats and no one really knows why the medievals were so fond of them as they represent so much labour. They were probably status symbols.

Out in the countryside, there are fine views and the tower of Radwinter Church can be glimpsed through a gap in the hedge. About a third-of-a-mile beyond New House Lane, turn right ⟹ along a 'no through' road, opposite an old green footpath sign. Once part of Ashdon Lane this is a delightful half-mile sunken lane, edged with mature and varied hedgerows of maple, hawthorn, hazel, dogwood, wild rose, wayfaring tree, spindle, willow and oak. The radio mast used by Essex Police is in a fenced enclosure.

Glimpsed through the hedge to the left, isolated from all intrusion, lies the old house of St. Aylotts, where legend has it that in some distant era 'Sainct Aylet was martered at a place bearing his name'. Could this be why the Abbot of Walden chose this distant spot, assarted out of Hales Wood in the mid-thirteenth century, a moated retreat, for his country home and chapel? As monasticism declined from pious to more secular needs, a later Abbot cut down 400 oaks to build the present fine house, precisely dated by dendochronology to 1500, but retaining the old moat. A recent survey has confirmed the importance of this grade one listed building, which was a farm from 1572.

St Aylotts, surrounded by beautiful ancient countryside of little fields, old hedges, pasture, meadow and woodland, must have abounded in wildlife.

Gibson, the Walden botanist, recorded the now rare Green-winged Orchid as common here in the last century. Stretching away into the distance, at the bottom of the lane is Hales Wood, a Site of Special Scientific Interest (SSSI) and the first National Nature Reserve to be established in Essex. Once it reached up to here, but now is slightly smaller. Great oak trees from Ashdon Hales were bought by the King from the Abbot in 1480, and used for rebuilding work at Kings' College Chapel, Cambridge.

Geographically Hales lies in Ashdon parish, and in 1790 the lord of Ashdon manor tried to claim it by putting up signposts, but Lord Braybrooke took legal action, for it was always part of the manor of Walden, and in the nineteenth century 'well-known to sporting characters... the rousing horn has awakened attention, year by year, at this extensive covert'.

Turn right ⇒ along a field-edge path, where can be seen a 'trig. point' at 390 feet above sea level – made redundant by satellite technology, these can now be 'adopted' from the Ordnance Survey. From here there is a fine view towards the Bartlow Hills.

This footpath is all that remains of a Roman road which went to the important Roman centre of Great Chesterford. Here, if anywhere, it should be possible 'to have felt back through the centuries', but two millennia have buried it all about 18 inches down and imagination fails as it looks just like any other field path. The enormous width of the road – something like 126 feet, more than a modern motorway – has long been absorbed into the fields. In 1849, however, some chalk and flint materials from the old road were noticed in a ditch along Wills Ayley Lane. Recent field-walking suggests there was plenty of farming in Roman times, but afterwards, 400 years of occupation faded as though it had never been, scrub and woodland reclaiming roads and farmland. But somehow this little bit of road survived, and centuries later parish boundaries evolved when old roads like these would be a natural place to mark with boundary trees and hedges. The well-known method of hedge-dating by counting species does not extend back to Roman times, but the average over ten 30-pace stretches is $4^{1}/_{2}$ which, if the theory works, suggests a Tudor planting.

Along here in May 1823, possibly for the last time since the Ordnance Survey was revolutionising map-making, the beating of the bounds was held to ensure these important boundaries remained clearly in oral memory, the Saffron Walden Corporation giving the town land surveyor John King five guineas for 'attending the parishioners for the purpose of showing the Bounds of the same parish.' Cross a footbridge into a large field once called Noakes after a long-gone farmer. Continue following the hedgerow until it bends away to the left and just here look for a cross-field path diagonally to the right ⇒ usually reinstated, but maybe unclear after ploughing.

At the far side, turn right ⇒ just a few paces to the double signposts by Wills Ayley Lane, now called New House Lane. Some of the buildings of the old farm, dating back to the sixteenth century, can be seen in the distance.

WALK 7: SEWARDS END

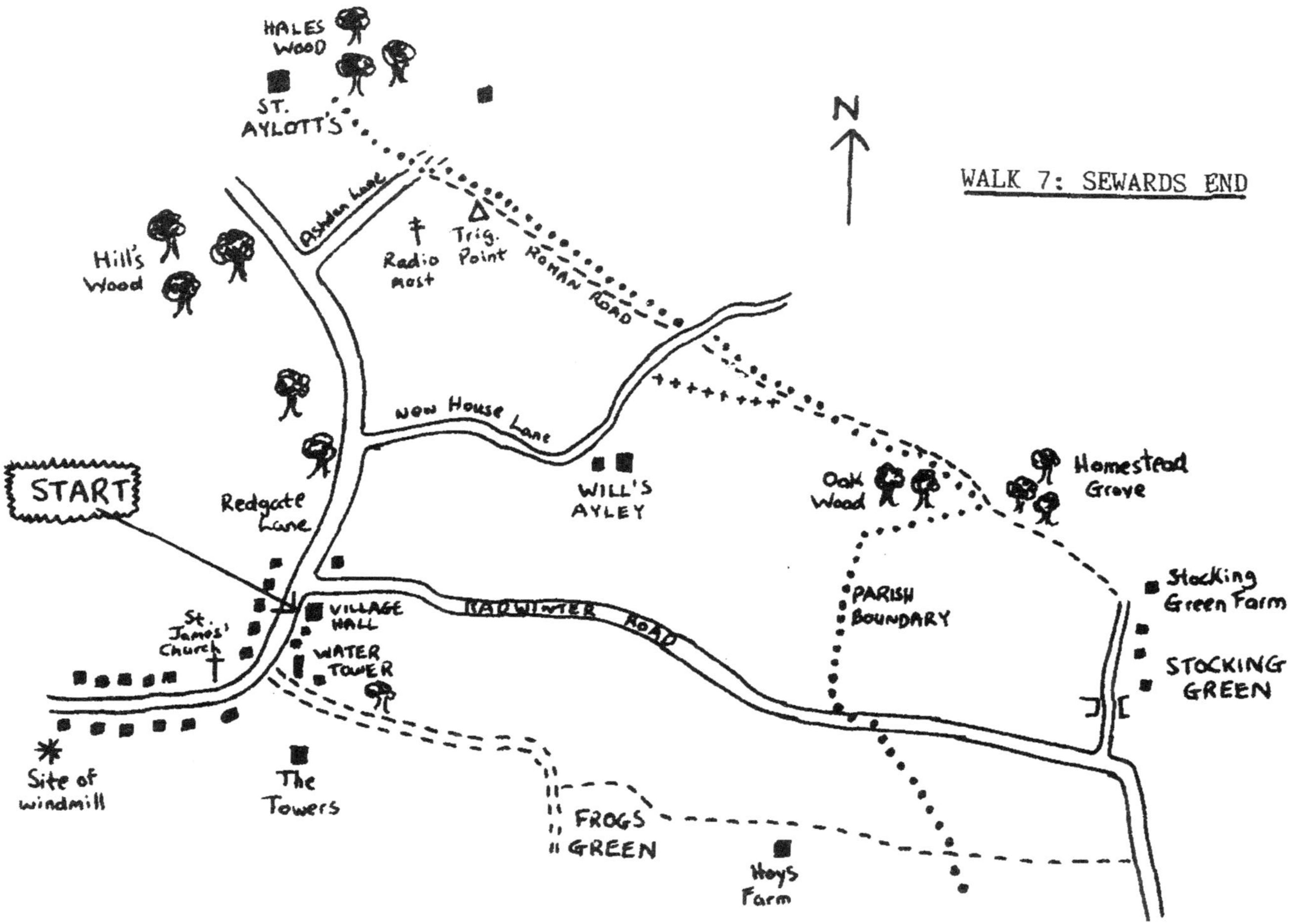

N

HALES WOOD

ST. AYLOTT'S

Hills Wood

START

Radio Mast

Trig. Point

ROMAN ROAD

WILL'S AYLEY

NEW HOUSE LANE

Redgate Lane

St. James' Church

Site of windmill

VILLAGE HALL

WATER TOWER

The Towers

RADWINTER ROAD

FROGS GREEN

Hoys Farm

Oak Wood

PARISH BOUNDARY

Homestead Grove

Stocking Green Farm

STOCKING GREEN

© Crown Copyright 85969M10/96

Near Wills Ayley

Wills Ayley may once have been bigger, even perhaps a small hamlet. The name links with that of a medieval farmer called William Ailly in 1377, but there is also a connection with the monks of St. Aylotts – the two names are similar, and it is suggested that the monks were particularly unpopular in these parts, through their laws and taxes. There *is* something eerie hereabouts, a feeling of history, but little to go on. Down Wills Ayley Lane, in the terrible winter of January 1895, a tramp was found frozen to death.

The Roman road route is sometimes hard to follow ahead through the crops, so an alternative recommended is to turn right ⇒ along the lane for about 100 yards, then left ⇐ along a waymarked path beside a ditch, which comes to the same place, after which keep ahead, still on the Roman road. Some years these are barley fields, reminiscent of the eighteenth and nineteenth centuries when malt had replaced saffron in the local economy, and Walden was a centre of the malting trade, with over 30 maltsters and brewers in the 1830s – the town smelt beery in those days! In spring there are Cowslips, in summer St. John's Wort, in winter the candy-pink poisonous fruits of spindle are noticeable. Spindle is seldom planted now, and is usually taken as a sign of an old hedge, one which had a particular use in times past, for the making of spindles. The tall hedgerow also provides songposts, encouraging for the beautiful summer visitor, yellowhammer, with the distinctive long note at the end of its song.

A little embanked green grove called Oakwood, also containing ash, maple and dogwood, is much smaller than it was in the last century. There are lots of pretty flowers along here and it is interesting to reflect on their herbal uses in former times – for Herb Bennet was a powerful charm against evil spirits, and Germander Speedwell was supposed to speed the well-being of patients while the strewing herb, Meadowsweet was used to sweeten mead and was an early source of aspirin. Just to the left, actually in the parish of Radwinter parish, some Roman tiles were once found, possibly the site of a tile kiln.

Go through a gap over the boundary, and keep ahead, by turning left then right to walk with Homestead Grove on the left, still on the Roman route. This grove may be ancient, as it is ditched and embanked, a superb wildlife habitat, darkly hidden behind a thick hedge wall where birds and squirrels and many other creatures live in peace. So can the walker on this quiet grassy track, sheltered from the weather, with views to open countryside, pondering all the things which have happened since this 2,000-year-old route came into being.

After the woodland thins out into a hedgerow, continue on towards the buildings of Stocking Green, the name derived from tree stumps, reflecting medieval woodland clearance hereabouts. In those times it was part of John de Mattens' sub-manor, rented out to peasant farmers. Turn right ⟹ at Stocking Green Farm past the tiny quiet hamlet of Stocking Green and over a white-railinged bridge to emerge on the Radwinter road.

Stocking Green

63

Here turn left ⇐ uphill for a few minutes – take care, it is very busy. By the Radwinter village sign turn right ⇒ on a wide, grassy bridleway. This is another splendid hedgerow, offering habitat to yellowhammers, finches and partridges; and shelter for wildflowers – Sweet Violets early in the year, Meadow Vetchling and Cinquefoil later with splashes of red Field Poppies enjoying bare patches. No plant has more names than Lords and Ladies or Cuckoo Pint or Parson-in-the-Pulpit – because of certain associations! Cross to the other side of the ditch, over the unseen parish boundary, along a shady track with fine views. An old hedgerow is regenerating alongside – many lost hedges could easily come back thus from their roots; another method of renewal is the regrowth from stumps, seen here in an old five-trunked ash coppice. Trees can virtually live forever if periodically coppiced. Veer right and left past Hoys Farm to emerge on a gravel track and turn left ⇐ for just a few yards past a waymark by a cottage, then immediately right ⇒ following the bridlepath sign.

The path passes a series of lovely oak trees, reminder of the ancient woodland of Keburdheys which flourished on what was damp, difficult land – when granted to Walden Abbey in the twelfth century, they complained that the land would grow nothing but 'nettles and sour weeds'. John Player, writing in the nineteenth century, repeated an old tale that 'one of a desperate gang of rogues was suspended in chains' in monastic times in Kebberdies – there must be some basis to these legends, but they get embellished in the telling. Kebberdies was part of the demesne, sold by Lord Braybrooke in 1814 during enclosure. Gradually farmers have cleared away the old woodland and improved the land, so it no longer grows only 'sour weeds'. A few ponds, wells and cottages are all that remains of former settlement, and all is quiet now, the path winding on beneath stately oaks, a breeze stirring the corn, Sewards End in the distance, but here a world apart. Emerge beside a signed bridlepath at Frogs Green, and here turn right ⇒ along another lovely green lane popular with rabbits. Someone once claimed to have seen, on a moonlit night, the ghosts of Cromwell's army on the march near Frogs Green, an association perhaps with Linton, where the so-called 'Battle of Saffron Walden' took place in 1648 not far away – the town did play a small but significant part in the Civil War. This lane had been a 'king's highway', the road to Wimbish and Radwinter, up to the Middle Ages. Today it remains a quiet and beautiful green lane, tree-lined with rampant pink dogrose clambering high in summer, followed by a harvest of hips. Nestling in a corner, among clouds of Queen Anne's Lace and waving grasses, is the blue splash of Lesser Periwinkle, a former woodland plant, none too common. Passing the tall treetops, a pair of green woodpeckers flash red and green, laughing. Behind the newer homes can be seen part of the four-towered folly of The Towers, once the home of an eccentric, later a public school, later still a wartime convalescent home for American officers.

The path emerges at a Coronation seat, by a water tower built in 1905, to solve the long-standing water supply problems of Sewards End caused by its being higher above sea level than Walden. The return to the village hall is to the right ⇒ but there are some interesting medieval houses in both directions, including Everards, Campions, Elms Farm(older than its pargetted date), Swans Cottage and Chapel Cottage, at its side once a Baptist chapel. Opposite the water-tower is the little chapel-of-ease, built by public subscription in 1847, on land given by William Gayton, owner of The Towers. Later there was a schoolroom for 90 pupils, including workhouse children who were marched here each day – by a strange irony, Gayton was bankrupted and ended his own days in the workhouse. Education and religion were part of the Victorian onslaught on the poverty and perceived heathenism of this little outpost. Missionaries from Walden organised barn services, saving souls, while lady visitors bearing food parcels might save a distressed family from starvation. People were kind, but few questioned the system which produced such dire poverty, and which persisted into living memory: when the last miller/baker was called up for service in the First World War, villagers unsuccessfully petitioned to keep him, relying on the use of his oven and the unsold bread he gave to poor families. The good old days?

Sewards End Mill, 1811 (J.M. Youngman)

Cloptons

8 Little Walden: 5 miles

Little Walden, Parva Waledene of 1248, is an outpost of the town, as is Sewards End, but much smaller. In medieval times it possessed that supreme status symbol, the deer park, quite a different concept from the landscape park of the eighteenth century. Scattered over the rest of the area, there were a lot more people settled than now and the landscape must have looked quite different – here in the last century the Frog Orchid could still be found in wet meadows, now no more. Today, though much changed, it remains a quiet area of damp upland, criss-crossed with streams and dotted with ponds, with many fine trees and hedgerows, and the occasional surprise of a stunningly beautiful old farmhouse. This is a lovely walk, 'away from all mankind'.

The Crown, Little Walden

Little Walden, its verges bright with massed crocus and snowdrops in spring, is a small, sleepy backwater which belies its history. Near the Hall Farm is said to be the line of a Roman road, and there is some evidence of transitory Roman settlement hereabouts – grave goods of the first and second century AD can be seen in Saffron Walden Museum.

The present Hall Farm dates to about 1800, with three barns and a fine brick wall also nearly 200 years old. Newer cottages have been built on plots which originated as smallholdings in medieval times, but there is at least one old house, Thatched Cottage, built around 1700.

Almost opposite the farm is a little church, remnant of Victorian concern for the spiritual welfare of the very poor labourers who lived here then. While Methodists held outdoor services here, and Congregationalists opened a chapel in a house opposite the pub, the Anglican church was actually paid for by a Quaker! In 1842, a missionary employed by Saffron Walden churches to visit the poor, reported that 'Little Walden is highly favoured, and the people of that place seem fully to appreciate their privileges'.

The eighteenth-century Crown Inn was formerly three cottages, and is very pleasant, with good food and hospitality to look forward to at the end of the walk. Turn left ⇐ from the pub past the Petlands estate, built to meet the post-war housing shortage, and presumably named from the field on which it stands, Perritt Land, which may derive from a Saxon word *pirige* meaning pear trees. The little village green once lay beside an old road, known at different times as Water, Freeborns or Park Lane, variously descriptive of its damp character, a past owner and the park to which it led. At some stage the present half-mile Petts Lane, formerly just a field boundary and now surfaced, seems to have become the favoured route and Water Lane abandoned to nature.

The cluster of dwellings is soon left behind, and the Madgate Slade, at whose head the hamlet was founded, has cut a surprisingly deep woody ravine, memento of earlier vigour when the water table was higher, for now it is often dry. The arable expanse to the right was medieval North feilde, one of the open fields, while to the left were little crofts named after past farmers, Wyberds and Falkeners and Clarkes. The distant woodland of Ashwells Grove adds an extra dimension to the three-layered greenery – flowery verge, its flora inherited from long-ago meads; streamside hedgerow of sloe and may, hazel and dogwood; and topping of chestnut, ash and maple, gnarled oaks of great age and old pollards of white willow.

The bend in the road once had a name, Jenkins Green, possibly a cottage site, now an untidy neglected corner, but this is just what wildlife likes best: for here is water in the form of two streams meeting in a pond; and here are feeding and breeding sites for butterflies in the form of nettles, sign of soil enriched by human activity; and here is cover from predators beneath the brambles: the wealth of birdsong in spring is eloquent testimony to a natural nature reserve. Pass the fishing lake and, at the top of the hill, the road goes on to Chesterford Park, but opposite the meeting point with Water Lane, turn right ⇒ through open metal gates to Home Farm, whence the fragrance of lilac is unmistakable in June. This must be a good place to live, not least because the residents seem to have a sense of humour!

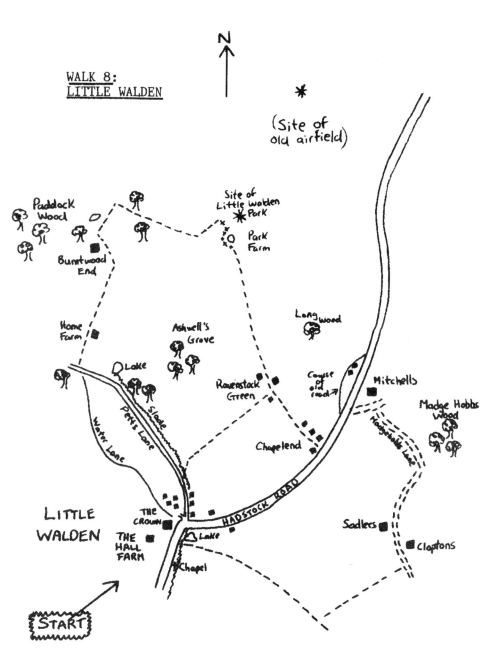

WALK 8:
LITTLE WALDEN

N

※ (Site of old airfield)

Paddock Wood

Burntwood End

Site of Little Walden Park

Park Farm

Home Farm

Ashwell's Grove

Lake

Slade

Long Wood

Ravenstock Green

Course of old road

Mitchells

Madge Hobbs Wood

Pett's Lane

Water Lane

Chapelend

HADSTOCK ROAD

LITTLE WALDEN

THE CROWN

THE HALL FARM

Lake

Chapel

Sadlers

Claptons

START

Beyond Home Farm grow meadow verges and, in a damp spot, the purple flowers of wild Comfrey, and everywhere trees and more trees – birches, willow, aspen and innumerable saplings in plastic tubes. It is as if someone is trying to replace lost hedgerows, diminished after the 1820s when 'lawless law's enclosure came', and the 1870s when agricultural depression took its toll on this ancient countryside. Old maps show a more intimate landscape of tiny hedged crofts and closes named after early farmers, Richards and Green, Smart and Rogers – a kind of immortality, but otherwise who were they all, these unknown toilers on the soil?

Burntwood End Farm

Mixed farming persisted into this century at Burntwood End, which had a granary, fowl house, pigsties, cow house, calf pens, cattle shed and loose boxes among its outbuildings. It is wonderful to wander up a path and come across a gem like Burntwood, early sixteenth-century – its name suggests how these marginal uplands were assarted from the forest. The timber-framed farmhouse, grade-one listed, blends into its surroundings of trees and ponds and animals. Oak grows well on these heavier soils – no doubt it was built with some such, like the huge specimen along by Burntwood, the size of which suggests it started life when Victoria came to the throne.

Wandering on, a wooded humpy area hides ponds, possibly sign of some old cottage here one time – the land may have been hard to work, but puddling ponds was easy on clay. Earlier this century there was by here an engine house pumping soft water by pipe from these ponds to the mansion in Chesterford Park. The works of man pass away, and nature takes over, painting sulphur hazel catkins in March and Bluebells in May, filling hedge-bottoms with Dog's Mercury and Cuckoo Pint, and damp hollows with Pendulous Sedge. Among the bushes in winter can be spotted the candy pink poisonous berries of spindle, curiously, for it prefers chalk. But the soil must be changing for the grassy verges support species like Salad Burnet – which is perfectly edible in salads – and Lady's Bedstraw – once used for stuffing mattresses, and Stitchwort, thought to cure the stitch – all once useful herbs. People love the ubiquitous Queen Anne's Lace – apparently known in Essex as Sheep Parsley – but so often it crowds out these more modest species.

For a few yards the path follows the ancient parish boundary of Walden before turning right ⇒ at the highest point, beside more plantations of plastic-encased saplings. Away to the left Paddock Wood hides a house-less moat, remnant of a medieval settlement, possibly older – there were some archaeological digs here in the 1970s.

Here is a glorious walk, a floral avenue between horse chestnuts: Cowslips, Knapweeds, Bedstraws, Willowherbs, Bryony, Birdsfoot Trefoil, Salad Burnet all fill the sunnier glades; butterflies flutter, drawn by nectar; roe deer flee the path; candled chestnuts throw dappled shade – stand beneath and look up into the branches. All is quiet. All is calm.

But moods change. A narrow overgrown path, entered after crossing a footbridge emerges onto a wider track between hedge and field and across another stream, and into the lonely outpost of old Little Walden Park, a creepy place even on a sunny day. For centuries this land was the hunting preserve of the lords of the Walden Manor, one of 150 deer parks in medieval Essex, a valuable resource for wood and meat. This entailed complex management to prevent deer browsing on young shoots, so the enclosed park was organised in 17 compartments, divided up with banks and coppices, felled in turn and the new growth fenced off against deer. In 1336, when owned by John de Bohun, it was said to be two leagues, possibly about six miles round. In 1529 Henry VIII granted 'our park of Walden in the hamlet of Little Walden' to his Chancellor, Thomas Audley, who lies in Walden Church, entombed in slate said to be 'as black as his heart'. It could well be that the royals who visited Audley End were taken a-hunting: in 1578 the Saffron Walden Corporation spent two shillings 'for mendynge the way at Little Walden Park', the same year that Elizabeth I came to Audley End.

But, as happened elsewhere, farmland became too valuable to be used for hunting and the park declined during the sixteenth century. An eighteenth century estate map still called it Reddeere Park, which is surprising since fallow were more suitable for such parks. The old hunting lodge survived longer, but much of its history was erased when the nearby airfield was developed during the last war, and most of the 25 buildings which existed at the turn of the century have disappeared – yet Little Walden Park was a sixteenth century house of considerable merit. When sold in the early twentieth century, there were over 500 acres of land attached. Today only a few ponds survive to bear witness to what has been.

Perhaps that accounts for the odd and lonely atmosphere, but there were strange happenings in later centuries too. Demolition hides a sordid Victorian tale of poverty, incest and mysterious death which emerged in an Assize trial of July 1897. Living incestuously in one tiny room – as was so common in those times of poverty – lived an old shepherd, his daughter and her two illegitimate children: there had been other illegitimate children, possibly his, who had died. Another small child was found dead in a wash-house. Nothing could be proved, but they went to prison for a year.

Almost half-a-century on Little Walden Park lay on the edge of the USAAF airfield, operational from 1942 until 1945 between here and Hadstock – now-demolished buildings once held their bombs and stores. Further north the flat cornfields of the old aerodrome remain strangely eerie, said to be haunted by the ghost of a headless young airman! But time has blurred memory, and really the wartime pilot is as vanished as the hunting lord of the Middle Ages and the tragic shepherd of Victorian times. And something beautiful emerged from it all – the Anglo-American Playing Fields in town are a fine memorial to those who flew from these fields to defend freedom.

There seem to be various ways around Park Farm – the current favourite seems to be to turn right ⇒ round a pond, and ahead on a cross-field path, normally reinstated through crops. Walk ahead across this field, over a stream and ahead on a grass track to pass a pile of rubble, presumably the site of an old cottage and, by a little coniferous plantation for pheasants, a pond, recently cleaned out, which probably represents the site of yet another cottage. How much more populated these lands were in earlier times. Serious decline set in during the 1870s when half the land north of Walden was neglected, with four smallholdings at Ravenstock Green fading away. There are still a few buildings, two sixteenth century, but once there was a thriving little community – old field names, Beneherds, Henhams, Sopers, Wakkes, Goodriches speak of past families. The name first appears in 1320 as William de Ravenstok, but medieval settlement often re-used old sites and a field here called Potshers may well refer to the finding of pottery sherds. (The path to the right can be followed as a short cut back to Little Walden).

Continue down what was Nether Street to Chapel End, where Chapel Croft once 'pertained to the Chappel of Little Walden, to the use of the parson', and where cottage meetings and evening services were still recorded in the last century. Cross the Hadstock road and turn left ⇐ a short distance up to a driveway. Traces of an ancient sunken trackway, a packhorse route, have been found between Chapel End and Monks Hall. The road to Linton was once notorious for its water-logged condition, and part of an old road must lie hidden among bushes across to the left.

Turn right ⇒ along a signposted drive past a colourful floral verge. Our reward for letting wildflowers grow is the beauty of butterflies – 1996 particularly noted as the best year ever for painted lady butterflies and there were many in the Walden countryside, having flown 600 miles from Africa to feast on our flora. The path passes Mitchells, an absolute picture in the sunshine, and by here, somewhat hidden in a bush, is one of the 1950s Urban District Council metal signposts, usefully pointing the way to Saffron Walden and Sewards End, a piece of footpath furniture well worth preserving.

Old signpost
near Mitchells

As often happens, the present seventeenth century house is a rebuilding on an earlier site, for in medieval times Mitchells had been, like Cloptons, Wills Ayley, Beares, Herberts, Swains and others one of the smallholdings leased out under a curious local system called wareland, some kind of tax arrangement. Its name links to John Michel, a witness to the 1300 Walden Charter. By Tudor times, Mitchells had built up into a substantial farm of 140 acres, while at the turn of this century it had enlarged to 300 acres, with cattle shed, chaff house, granary, cart shed and piggeries, still pursuing a mixed farming system. There is still a large pond, with multifarious waterfowl.

Mitchells has a link with a turbulent period of English history, for in the seventeenth century its then owner, Charles Parris was one of those who suffered anti-Catholic persecution, accused of 'popish recusancy'. His estates including Bowsers in Ashdon and Mitchells were confiscated, but restored to the family after he died. Parris actually lived in Norfolk, but the Victorian writer, John Player, recalled another chap who did live here, a real local character – 'Adams of Mitchells... we miss the good man on juries, in the market, and on the road... his blue coat and gilt buttons.. the distinguishing attire peculiar at that period to the lord of Mitchells.'

Turn right ⇒ before the pond, near a spot to the left once a cottage called Oldharlwyns, long gone; but Madgehobs wood and lane survive, the name meaning tussocky meadow. This gentle downhill track is another of the ancient ways, who knows how old, linking for centuries the farms of Mitchells, Cloptons, Butlers, St Aylotts and Sewards End. This countryside perhaps lacks the wilder beauties of Burntwood but is still delightful. Veer right to pass round the back of old barns at Sadlers, another medieval wareland holding with a pond and some surviving medieval hedgerows, but with a mid-sixteenth century house. Although it started out with just ten acres, Sadlers also expanded through buying up extra land. In the last century Sadlers was one of many farms in this part of Essex targeted by angry labourers using incendiarism as their only weapon – in February 1851 a barn full of oats was set on fire. During the last war both Sadlers and the next farm along, Cloptons, were commandeered by the Government to grow essential crops.

Once again, Cloptons took its name from a fourteenth century smallholder, and a name of the field opposite, Plush Breeches, describes the process of early farming, translating as damp land, newly broken-in. Clopton's early building was replaced in 1643 by the present fine house, now attractively landscaped with an arched bridge. It takes the breath away, wandering along some old byway, to glance across a farmgate and see, framed between tall hedgerows, such a scene of rural charm.(see page 66)

From here the path, still following a route at least 600 years old, acquires a shadier, hedgier character and continues ahead to Butlers. Instead, turn right ⇒ over a plank bridge to a good field-edge path which follows a post-enclosure boundary, beneath sheltering oak, with extensive views. To the left were once the tiny patches of medieval smallholders, immortalised on old maps as Mottes and Ballandine and Herds, although the latter survived until the depression of the 1870s. Vanished too is old Almshouse Wood which was still here earlier this century, to the right of a wide cross-field path.

Turn right ⇒ downhill on the fertile valley slope, leaving behind the heavier uplands. Cutting through old Croft feld, one of Little Walden's four open fields, it may be that this grassy path, dotted with wild flowers, originated as a baulk between the strips cultivated in common under that complex system.

At dusk on a late winter's afternoon, the sun setting ahead in the western sky, the Walden woods distant dark shapes and the welcoming lights of the old Crown Inn down in the valley, it may be that a wheeling, falling, calling skylark forms momentarily a poignant link with the many long-forgotten souls who laboured their lives away on these old common lands.

Old field-gate near Cloptons

AshdonVillage Sign

9 Ashdon: 2½ miles

Only a few miles from Walden, the lovely village of Ashdon is a rambler's dream, with a network of over a hundred rights-of-way. This circular walk is short but goes right round Ashdon on good paths through a different sort of countryside, of steep fields and thick hedgerows, of meadows, woods and deeply-cut valley, as well as arable fields on both boulder clay and chalk.

Start at All Saints Church, fourteenth century, but on the same site as an earlier church – pagan burials have been found nearby. Inside is all the quiet charm of the best English village churches, cool and clean and unfussy: most of its riches were plundered after the Reformation but the Norman font-bowl survived. There is a story that the altar rails were restored in 1927 after being used for almost 50 years as henhouse perches. Such things are valued all the more for being temporarily mislaid. Likewise there was joy when the bells peeled forth in 1969 after being out of repair for 90 years.

**Ashdon
Church**

Outside in the churchyard, 'all the air a solemn stillness holds', and it is pretty with waving wild grasses, offering living habitat as well as resting place. From behind the church can be seen the timber-framed, medieval 'Gilde Aule de Asshendon', a beautiful building whose chequered history reflects the vicissitudes of government: when Henry VIII abolished religious guilds, it became a poorhouse, later with 25 poor folk living here and working at spinning in the eighteenth century. But when the official mood changed again in the 1830s, the village poor were carted off to the hated, impersonal Union in Walden, and the old guildhall became residential.

To the left of the church is a field said to be the site of the deserted medieval village of old Ashdon, which fell into silence after the Plague in 1348, when the present village centre emerged. There is disagreement among academics though – thirteenth century pottery and sunken tracks, the finding of weapons and animal bones, show there was some great significance in Home Meadow. But the bumps could be ancient vineyard terraces, or possibly just the hollows of old diggings – careless nineteenth century gravel diggers destroyed evidence. It may be the mystery field has some connection with the significant Battle of Assendun of 18 October 1016, even that the victorious Danish army of Cnut might have camped here. After all it was Holinshed, no less, in his sixteenth century Chronicle who stated that King Edmund 'hasted foorth to succour his people, and at Ashdone in Essex three miles from Saffron Walden, gave battell to Cnute...'

From the church door, turn right ⇒ through a gap in the fence and over a stile. Bear right across Home Meadow to another stile, then left ⇐ but immediately right ⇒ to cross the stream on a high causeway, past an overgrown area once a gravel pit. Over to the right is Pond Bay, said to be the site of a medieval stewpond or fishpond. All is now tumbled back to nature with tall Teasels, Mugwort and other wild plants. Even more delightful is the flora of the field track, skirted in summer by a verge full of colourful wildflowers – blue Scabious and white Bladder Campion, pink Clover and purple Hardheads, with red Field Poppies and waving grasses of green and gold. Dogroses of palest pink climb the hedgerows and above them the lark celebrates the freedom of this beautiful landscape of flowing hill and shallow valley – behind to the church, distantly left to Goldstones, and away right to Little Hales Wood where many a gang of men in poorer times caught their dinner on a dark winter's night. Poaching was a way of life in Ashdon, with so many tempting woodlands about. Almost a tenth of Ashdon parish was woodland one time.

Passing hedges, into the next field, through another hedge, the path turns left ⇐ on a walkable field-edge beside a hedge of hawthorn. The heavier clay of this side of the parish can make it heavy going in wet seasons. But it's a pleasant downhill trek through a gap over a rather wobbly stile into a long, narrow slipe of a meadow, then over a step-stile into a bigger meadow, and continuing down to a little footbridge.

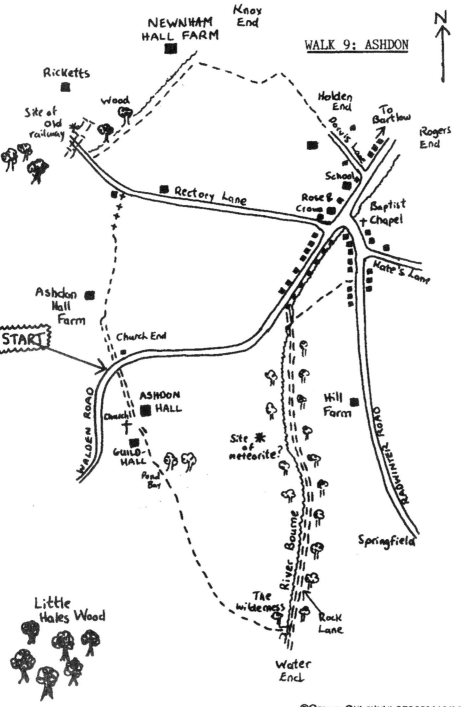

Newnham Hall Farm
Knox End
Ricketts
Wood
Site of old railway
WALK 9: ASHDON
N
Holden End
Davis Lane
To Bartlow
Rogers End
School
Rectory Lane
Rose & Crown
Baptist + Chapel
Kate's Lane
Ashdon Hall Farm
START
Church End
Holden Road
Church
ASHDON HALL
GUILD-HALL
Pond Bay
Site of meteorite?
Hill Farm
RADWINTER ROAD
River Bourne
The Wilderness
Rock Lane
Springfield
Water End
Little Hales Wood

©Crown Copyright 85969M10/96

Hazel in the hedges is a picture of sulphur yellow in spring, and it is good to hear the rookery noisily from the treetops, for rooks are not as common as they once were. Here, dividing the parish in two, is the little Bourne, its name meaning 'river river', and the reason why a settlement grew up here. Downstream it gathers water from the hills, becomes the Granta and eventually joins the Cam which goes through Cambridge. Below 'green and deep the stream mysterious glides beneath', seeming too mild to have cut this deep ravine, but the water table was higher in earlier times, and perhaps it was deepened for watermills. Nearby is Water End, where Baptists used to hold open air services in the 1900s.

Go over the river on a solid railed footbridge across to an area laid out for equine pursuits – turn left ⇐ along here, a nice woody area left to nature. Big yellow bracket fungi find a niche in the piles of old logs left for wildlife – too often these are tidied up and a valuable resource lost. There are squirrels doing acrobatics in the treetops, and butterflies in the glades. This field, once a marshy meadow, now drained, is known as The Wilderness, and is a delightful natural area.

Turn left ⇐ over a high stile to a waymarked bridleway, past Moor Cottage with its attractive garden, towards another waymark post beside a former chicken house. A footpath on the right leads up to Springfield which early in the century was the experimental site of Ashdon's fruit farming tradition. This woody track is an old green way called Rock Lane, originally linking Ashdon with Walden via Redgates Lane at Sewards End. This is the best bit, a sheltered streamside stroll, serenaded by birdsong and breezes, high above the little Bourne, where there used once to be a watermill. The path shows signs of recent improvement works, but not to the detriment of the tangled underwood enjoyed by a myriad creatures, and dampness enjoyed by Pendulous Sedge and wild Comfrey, the miraculous knitbone herb.

Picturesque cottages with pretty gardens lie at intervals along the Bourne. Somewhere over to the left, on 9th March 1923, a meteorite weighing 44 ounces landed making a two-foot dent in a cornfield and frightening the life out of a farmworker nearby. It was heard as far away as Saffron Walden, where there is a copy in the Museum, the original being unusual enough to find home in the Natural History Museum. Possibly Rock Lane got its name from that extraordinary artefact from outer space? Strange things happen in Ashdon. Ten years earlier the most ferocious hailstorm imaginable had ripped through the village, breaking every window with huge lumps of ice. Continue ahead on a signposted bridleway beside which 'the water is cool, gentle and brown, above the pool', where tiddlers sport in sunny shallows. Those who know the river speak of finding trout in secret places. Trees offer many wildlife niches, from the tops of their branches where the songbirds call, to their old gnarled roots in the bank where rabbits burrow and bees dig little holes. In the sunnier spots are ordinary pretty things, flowering grasses attracting butterflies, and the ubiquitous little pink Herb Robert. A green archway of fallen trees leans in old age against an even older pollard, decorated with bracket fungi, a piece of natural woodland sculpture.

Glimpsed through trees is Hilly Meadow, climbing to Hill Farm, which currently houses the Ashdon Museum, a fascinating collection of bygones. What is it about this parish, a special something, which touches people? Its ingredients seem simple enough – the Victorian writer, John Player, said Ashdon in 1845 had plenty of 'hills and dells, water-courses and umbrageous retreats' but was otherwise undistinguished. Yet others have more accurately found it 'no ordinary village'.

The wayside weeds, pernicious elsewhere, seem beautiful in Ashdon – tall and stately Spear Thistles, luscious butterfly-Nettles, Sticky Willy clambering over a tree stump. Even Ground Elder, foolishly imported as a pot herb by the Romans, transforms into a stately clump of creamy-white flowers when allowed to do its own thing.

The lovely lane ends all too soon, crossing over two bridges made of railway sleepers, into a meadow and through a gap in the hedge. In June the warm sloping home meadows smell of sweet new-mown hay, calling to mind that long ago summer of 1914 when the hay harvest lay rotting, for all the Ashdon farmworkers were on strike, seeking to increase their thirteen shillings weekly wage. An old oak stump, thoughtfully left in the meadow, would have been a mature tree then. There are some lovely trees at the top of field, beside a fine tiled barn and timbered Tudor Croft, with notable chimneys.

Cross the field diagonally to emerge on the Radwinter Road opposite Kate's Lane, an eighteenth century name – once this formed the boundary with a separate hamlet, Steventon. A militia sword from the Napoleonic Wars, found in Kates Lane, is a proud possession of Ashdon Museum. Turn left ⇐ through the village centre, rich in old cottages, of timber, plaster, red or yellow brick, pegtiles and slate, sometimes thatch. The old police house is well named; the legend of Dick Turpin gets reference; there is a 300-year-old former bakery, an old bootmakers' now 'Maltings', and a former butchery now 'Willow Cottage'.

Meeting places, past and present cluster round the junction: the present village hall; nineteenth century Baptist Chapel, replacing the dilapidated old barn at nearby Chapel Farm; and the last two pubs, the Old Fox now residential, and the Rose and Crown still thriving. The Rose and Crown, noted for its seventeenth century wall paintings, has been a pub for over 200 years – the men loved it for its speciality brew, a strong porter known as 'entire', and for the women Crown Hill was also a meeting place for gossip round the pump. Here one time the vestry met to organise the minutiae of village life – doles to the poor, repairs to the roads.

The Fox, which closed in the 1960s after 140 years, had a well-known publican, who lived to a ripe old age, and doubled up as parish clerk, schoolmaster and village constable.

The Rose & Crown
Ashdon

In a field behind the Fox, the Ashdon strikers held concerts in the summer of 1914, singing the 'Red Flag' to piano and accordion accompaniment. Their public meetings also took place in the village centre. At least one confrontation took place in front of the Rose and Crown, and there was trouble everywhere – broken farmgates, burned haystacks, blocked roads. On one occasion they marched to Saffron Walden and back, forks and hayrakes on their shoulders. They won their fifteen shillings, just in time to save the harvest – and to march off to the trenches of France.

Turn right ⇒ at the junction, once called the 'three-went way', past the lovely gardens of Juniper House. The public well used to be along here – in 1688 the inhabitants of Ashdon were summonsed for not enclosing it. This is where Ashdon keeps its treasures – a Silver Jubilee seat of 1977; the garden war memorial, with the names of 'many a lightfoot lad' who never came back to Ashdon; trophies from some distant best-kept village competition – the trophy from a more recent win in 1988 is kept outside the village hall ; and a very well-made village sign, showing the ash tree after which the Domesday Ascenduna was named, amid a pastoral scene from the past, blending into the present background of hedges and fields(see page 76).

Cross the road opposite the splendid Victorian village school dating back to 1878, its clock always useful to villagers. Turn left ⇐ up a little old winding lane, Dorvis Lane, possibly named after John Dover, who owned land here a long time ago. A house in the lane, known as Aylewards, a former shop, has an unusual spiral staircase, and dates back to medieval times. The former Manse had an old pond, the Lady Well, said to be haunted by the ghost of a lady who drowned when lightning frightened her horses.

Passing the last cottage, go through the gate, closing it carefully as there may be stock in the meadow. At one time Dorvis Lane continued beyond the gate, hence the high bank may be the lynchet of the old lane. This is a fine spacious meadow dotted with oaks, populated by rabbits, with views of distant wooded hills. Ashdon is full of separate 'ends' – Knox End, Church End, Water End. Holden End nearby was a centre for strawplaiting in the last century when about 20 families lived there. Ignore the stiled footbridge, beside which is a large sarsen stone, remnant of an ice age millions of years ago. Unfortunately there is no view of the famous Roman burial mounds, the curious Bartlow Hills.

Follow the track alongside a fence, then through a farm gate to pass Newnham Hall Farm, built on a sheltered, streamside site in the sixteenth and seventeenth centuries, but replacing an earlier building nearby, one time known as Cloptons after its medieval owners. It is many centuries since it was new, for at Domesday 'Neunham' belonged to one of William the Conqueror's right-hand men, and at one time the manorial lands spread right across the parish. The thirteenth century lord of the manor had the right to erect his own gallows, and hold assize of bread and ale. There were sheepwalks here one time for the chalk soil, though easier to work, was not as fertile as the claylands elsewhere. Today Newnham is part of the vast Vestey landholdings.

There are ghost stories round here, legends of fighting men seen on moonlit nights in distant fields, related perhaps to the Civil War battle at Linton which is not far away. A hoard of silver coins hidden at this time was found in 1984, a short distance away near Walton Hall. Skirt the left edge of the farmyard past the byre and silage area to a somewhat hidden stile on the right between tyres and machinery; but take care as the path is narrow and the stile slippery. Over to the left can be seen The Rectory, one of the finest houses in Ashdon. The path along the field is ploughed close and it is hard to find the track to the right ⇒ through the woods. But persevere as this is a lovely little Bluebell and oak woodland apparently called The Brues, with signs of fox as well as pheasant. Both wood and field paths emerge on an old high-banked lane, very near where the high-arched bridge of the Bartlow branch line used to cross: labourers working in the fields told the time by means of its four daily trains. There were dreams of linking further afield, but nothing came of it and then the whole railway got Beechinged anyway in the 1960s. Signs of Neolithic man have been found in the past hereabouts.

Turn left ⇐ up steep Rectory Lane, looking back to another little woodland and a pink house to the right called Ricketts. Turn right ⇒ at 'Westview' on a signposted path up a driveway to a newly-surfaced farm road. Look for a waymarked gap up the bank, and cross here to the other side of the hedge. Foxes can be spotted hereabouts. Mind the stinging nettles, in summer black with the caterpillars of tortoiseshell butterflies.

After passing some old farm implements, keep to the right along the side of a paddock, then right again ⇒ to the driveway of Hall Farm – this was the farm linked to Ashdon Hall, one of four ancient manors of the parish. Then turn left ⇐ back down to Church Hill, passing a flinted building which used to be the nineteenth century Ashdon National School, remaining in use till the village board school opened. Opposite is Ashdon Hall whose lovely gardens, lawns and moat are out of sight. The other big house in Ashdon, Waltons has another walk to be recommended.

In fact there is fine walking everywhere in Ashdon, enjoyed by the village walking group, continuing a tradition started by the late Dorothy Homewood, after whom one of the Ashdon paths is named. Like the footpath association of Saffron Walden, they have discovered the free therapy and enormous interest of the countryside which lies on their own doorstep. As John Player observed over 150 years ago: 'Travelling folk in search of the picturesque very often go a great number of miles to see places not nearly so interesting after all, as their own'.

Ashdon walkers

Final Thoughts

> "Why faintest thou? I wander'd till I died.
> Roam on! the light we sought is shining still.
> Dost thou ask proof? Our tree yet crowns the hill
> Our Scholar travels yet the loved hillside.'
>   Matthew Arnold

Highway Code

'Walkers should always take extra care on busy roads round Walden...'

Country Code

Take nothing but photographs
Leave nothing but footprints
Kill nothing but time

Sources of Information

Bibliography and full references for this book can be consulted at Saffron Walden Town Library. Principal sources marked with an asterisk.

William Addison, *Audley End*: useful background on the Braybrookes.

Patrick Armstrong, *The Changing Landscape*: readable study of East Anglia.

*Steven Bassett, *Saffron Walden: Excavations and Research* 1972-80: report on recent archaeological findings in the town.

Janet Clark, *Disaster at The Park*: excellent piece of oral history research.

English Heritage: *The Gardens of Audley End*: beautifully-produced, fascinating.

*John Field, *English Field Names: A Dictionary*: helps interpret field-names.

*Fitter, Fitter and Blamey, *The Wild Flowers of Britain and Northern Europe*: good guide for beginners to wild flower identification.

Robert Gibson, *Annals of Ashdon: No Ordinary Village*: readable, interesting.

*Angela Green, *Ashdon: A History of an English Village*: accurate, comprehensive.

Jean Gumbrell, *Favourite Haunts in and around Saffron Walden*: local ghost stories.

W.G. Hopkins, *The Making of the English Landscape*: explanation of how to interpret the features of the countryside: classic, pioneering, a wonderful read.

*Stanley T. Jermyn, *Flora of Essex*: sites and habitats of all plants in the county.

*Dorothy Monteith, *Saffron Walden and its Environs: A Study in the Development of a Landscape*: much-quoted pioneering study of town and local countryside.

P. Paye, *The Saffron Walden Branch*: meticulously-researched railway history.

*John Player, *Sketches of Saffron Walden and its Vicinity*: the original book of walks round Walden, interesting topographical descriptions 150 years ago.

Pollard, Hooper and Moore, *Hedges*: classic, how to date hedgerows.

*Oliver Rackham, *The History of the Countryside*: brilliant, detailed, highly readable explanations on woodlands, parks, fields, highways, pits, ponds, hedges, etc.

*Saffron Walden Antiquarian Society: *History* journal (various): useful record of researches by local historians.

Saffron Walden Museum: *Saffron Walden Local History Activity Guide*: very attractive and interesting summary of many aspects of town.

The Victoria County History of Essex: various academic studies of Saffron Walden.

*Malcolm White, *Saffron Walden: A Chronological Compilation*: a most useful gathering together of all previous studies of the town.

Tom Williamson, Article in *Essex Archaeology & History*, vol.17(1986): pioneering field-walking research on the antiquity of farming in N.W. Essex.

PRIMARY

*Estate maps of Saffron Walden for 1750s (Essex Record Office)

The Field Book of Walden, 1605 (Town Library)

Saffron Walden Town Archives (Saffron Walden Town Council

Useful Contacts

****

PROOFREADING: Also Word Processing (on disk, Word 6): articles/ books/ theses: contact 24 Pelham Road, Clavering, Essex CB11 4PQ.

****

ILLUSTRATION: Numbered prints of charcoal drawings : Julie Lynne, 1288 Boiling Springs Road, Boiling Springs, Pennsylvania 17007, USA.

****

GRAPHIC DESIGN: Typesetting, disk conversion, scanning. John Hills, Gemini Graphics, Sawbridgeworth (01279 722627.

****

PRINTING: Local self-published books a speciality, reasonable rates, personal service: Alan Hawkins, Print Matters (01279-302095).

****

INFORMATION on Saffron Walden: Tourist Information Centre, situated in the Market Square, open weekdays (01799-510444)

****

SAFFRON WALDEN MUSEUM open daily, excellent displays on local history, wildlife and other themes. Museum Street (01799-510333)

****

LOCAL HISTORY CENTRE in Town Library: extensive research sources. Open weekdays except Wednesday, Market Square. (01799-523178)

****

ARCHIVE ACCESS (Essex Record Office): primary sources on N.W. Essex on microfilm. Town Hall, Market Square (01799-516821)

****

LOCAL SOCIETIES welcome new members: Essex Wildlife Trust, Family History Society, Historical Society, Museum Society, Town Library Society. Contacts from Tourist Information Centre.

****

FOOTPATH WALKS: Organised regularly by the Saffron Walden Footpath Association: contact telephone number from Tourist Information Centre.

****

GUIDED TOURS offered by Uttlesford Blue Badge Guides, Saffron Walden and local area. Contact from Tourist Information Centre.

****

SEWARDS END VILLAGE HALL: new, purpose-built hall available for lettings: contact telephone number from Tourist Information Centre.

****

SAFFRON WALDEN YOUTH HOSTEL: inexpensive, comfortable accommodation for walkers, in old maltings. (01799-523117)

****